Intellectual Giftedness in Young Children: Recognition and Development

The *Journal of Children in Contemporary Society* series:

Intellectual Giftedness in Young Children: Recognition and Development

Edited by
Joanne Rand Whitmore, PhD

The Haworth Press
New York • London

Intellectual Giftedness in Young Children: Recognition and Development has also been published as *Journal of Children in Contemporary Society*, Volume 18, Numbers 3/4, Spring/Summer 1986.

The Haworth Press, Inc., 12 West 32 Street, New York, NY 10001
EUROSPAN/Haworth, 3 Henrietta Street, London WC2E 8LU England

Library of Congress Cataloging-in-Publication Data

Intellectual giftedness in young children.

"Has also been published as Journal of children in contemporary society,
volume 18, numbers 3/4, spring/summer 1986"—T.p. verso.
   Bibliography: p.
   Includes index.
   1. Gifted children—United States—Identification. 2. Gifted children—Education
(Primary)—United States. 3. Problem children—Education (Primary)—United States.
I. Whitmore, Joanne Rand, 1938-   . [DNLM: 1. Child Development. 2. Child, Gifted.
W1 JO584T v.18 no. 3/4 / WS 105 I595]
LC3993.9.I58 1986   371.95   86-19374
ISBN 0-86656-540-X

Intellectual Giftedness in Young Children: Recognition and Development

Journal of Children in Contemporary Society
Volume 18, Numbers 3/4

7119068

CONTENTS

APPENDIXES

Preface

For many decades it has been an accepted fact that the early years of life critically influence the development of the child's emotional and social characteristics as well as intellectual abilities. Although theorists and researchers have offered diverse conceptions of the "critical" age period and the extent to which the environment influences child development, all have agreed the first eight years of life are most important. It is during those early years that patterns of feeling, perceiving, and behaving are developed to form the child's self-concept, personal motivations, and perceptions of the environment which critically affect the development of specific abilities.

Within the last two decades, Americans have reflected their confidence in these facts about early development by supporting Federal legislation and the funding of projects to offset the negative effects of environments severely limiting the potential growth of children (specifically, the economically disadvantaged, culturally different, and handicapped populations). Federal projects such as Head Start have demonstrated the effectiveness of early intervention to guide the optimal development of a young child's attitudes and abilities. It has been only in recent years, however, that similar concerns have been raised relative to the special needs of young gifted children (birth to age 8). With increasing frequency, conscientious parents are asking professionals what they ought to do about the observed educational needs of their young children (e.g., early interest in reading, intense drives to complete complex projects, a tendency to play only with much older children) and the desirability of systematic home instruction and preschool or daycare options.

This publication has been created in response to the concerns expressed by many parents and early childhood educators. Its primary purpose is to provide parents and teachers of young children, as well as other human services professionals, with concise, accurate, and helpful information in response to common questions and relevant issues. The need for such a publication has been created by the fact that the latest thinking and understandings often do not filter down to the actual child caregivers. Libraries contain many books with outdated conceptions or information that may mislead the inquiring

xi

adult. Additionally, there is much controversy in current popular literature regarding the extent to which parents should systematically try to accelerate the development of the infant-toddler; some professionals lead parents to believe that intense instruction during that period can make the youngster become gifted. Teachers are equally vulnerable to misconceptions about giftedness and to a lack of accurate information as a result of professional preparation programs that fail to include the knowledge and instructional skills necessary for them to make appropriate educational provisions for gifted children.

The contributing authors for this publication were selected for their leadership in the field of early education of intellectually gifted children. All of them have contributed significantly to our growing knowledge about the special needs of young gifted children, blending their understanding of the latest theories and research with their practical experience as educators and clinicians. All of them have demonstrated an exceptional ability to translate defensible theories into effective educational practice through their successful provision of services to parents, children, and families. Specific information about the authors will be included in the introduction to each section and article.

In order to provide a concise publication on a topic of such significance and complexity, it was imperative that the authors carefully select the most relevant and important information needed to inform the practices of parents and teachers. The topic, therefore, has been addressed in four parts, corresponding to the most common questions and areas of new information and insight: The Nature of Intelligence and Giftedness; Recognizing Intellectual Giftedness in Young Children; Effective Ways of Nurturing the Development of Intellectual Giftedness; and Special Needs and Educational Issues. Each part will contain an introduction to the issues relevant to the section and articles written by two authorities in the field of gifted education. A list of pertinent references and additional resources will be found following the Summary and Conclusions.

Joanne Rand Whitmore, PhD
Guest Editor

Intellectual Giftedness in Young Children: Recognition and Development

PART I:
THE NATURE OF INTELLIGENCE AND GIFTEDNESS

Introduction

Historically gifted individuals have been defined as those who achieve or perform at exceptionally high levels of success and who possess "a high IQ" as measured on a standardized test of intellectual aptitude. In recent years, however, we have refined our conception of giftedness to acknowledge that there are gifted individuals in any area of human endeavor. Those recognized as gifted generally acquire particular skills and/or knowledge with exceptional ease and speed, and evidence their giftedness in the qualitatively superior outcomes of their efforts in the area(s) of their giftedness. We judge the individual's exceptionality or giftedness by comparing his/her achievements and quality of products with others of the same age, generally regarding the child as gifted when his/her performance is superior to 90, 95, or 99% of the age population. Thus, gifted children are considered to be in the top one, three, five, or ten (sometimes even twenty) percent of the total population in quality of performance on a fair standard measure of that ability. Most often the only reason for selecting a certain percentage is the number of children funded programs can serve.

As an outgrowth of concern in the 1960s and 1970s about providing educational programs to fully develop the abilities of "disadvantaged" and "handicapped" children, we became aware of the importance of focusing on *potential* rather than just demonstrated ability. As a consequence, the Federal definition of giftedness was expanded to include potential for high achievement, and the content of the Congressional Marland Report (1972) allowed for the inclusion of underachievers in the gifted population. The old "Nature vs. Nurture" debate was subsequently revived and continues, with most discussions acknowledging the importance of both the child's genetically inherited "potential" and the environmental nurturance of that potential so that it becomes manifested in high achievement.

A simple, practical definition of giftedness, generally acceptable to all theorists, is *the manifestation of exceptional potential for high achievement in the area(s) of giftedness.* It is important to specify the area of giftedness when referring to students (e.g., intellectually gifted, musically talented, creatively gifted). Just as there are gifted individuals in any area of human ability, there also are specific kinds of giftedness within each of those areas. For example, an individual gifted or talented in art is not apt to be equally exceptional in potential as a sculptor, oil painter, watercolor artist, nor will others expect the person to be equally superior in portraying human figures, animals, landscapes, impressionistic drawings and abstract designs. In referring to the intellectually gifted children in our schools, however, we tend to expect superior motivation and achievement in every area of the curriculum, in all kinds of intellectual activity.

It is more accurate to designate the specific kind(s) of intellectual giftedness possessed by students who do not manifest a broad, general form of intellectual superiority (e.g., mathematically gifted, scientifically gifted, or verbally gifted). Furthermore, intellectually gifted students will have varying degrees of ability or giftedness across specific mental abilities. For example, some will be more talented in analytical and logical thinking than in divergent, creative production; some will be avid readers, some poor readers; some will be highly motivated consumers of factual knowledge while others will tend to be weak on factual recall and thrive on creative idea play, the generation of new insights. Guilford's theoretical construct of more than 120 specific mental abilities comprising intelligence suggests the need to be very specific in identifying high levels of aptitude within individuals and to avoid overgeneralized expectations, especially with regard to the intellectually gifted children we seek to identify and serve in most school programs.

This is a very exciting time in the history of the field of gifted education. Many new theories and research findings regarding the psychology of intelligence and giftedness are giving us new insights, explanations, and directions to guide our parenting and teaching. Two of the most provocative and promising researchers/theorists are Howard Gardner and Robert Sternberg. Gardner (1983) has stimulated our thinking about the existence and development of multiple intelligences in children. Sternberg has analyzed intelligence as information processing to suggest specific components of intelligence that refine our conception of giftedness as well as intelligence. His book, *Beyond IQ* (1985), broadens our thinking about intelligence to the specific cognitive processes that discriminate kinds of intelligence and may discriminate the intellectually gifted from the nongifted. His new book, *Conceptions of Giftedness* (1986), specifically addresses our need for more precise definitions and understandings of giftedness. In addition to creative theorists like Gardner and Sternberg, there is much promise in the efforts of groups such as the New York Foundation for Brain Research[1] which is attempting to increase discourse and collaboration among researchers to explore the functions of the brain in relation to intelligence and the nature of giftedness.

The two contributing authors of this section address the characteristics of intellectually gifted children as established by research and tested in successful professional practice. Barbara Clark has become recognized internationally for her application of the most recent brain research to effective education of gifted children. In addition to her two editions of *Growing Up Gifted* (1979, 1983), she has a 1986 book that more fully explicates her use of Integrative Education to nurture the full development of cognitive potential. Her article will highlight the most significant knowledge from brain research and implications for defining and nurturing intellectual giftedness. Wendy Roedell will address the noncognitive attributes of gifted children, the social and emotional characteristics that make them vulnerable to difficulties and create a need for guidance and affective education. She will draw from her experiences as director of the Child Development Preschool for Gifted Children at the University of Washington as well as other professional work.

FOOTNOTE

1. For further information contact Miles Storfer, President (85-86), The Foundation for Brain Research, P.O. Box 104, Cooper Station, New York, NY 10276.

Early Development of Cognitive Abilities and Giftedness

Barbara Clark, EdD

ABSTRACT. With advances in technology, there is now a better understanding of the organization and function of the human brain. The result has been a challenge to many of the beliefs previously held regarding learning, intelligence and giftedness. Neither intelligence nor giftedness can now be viewed as only the result of cognitive functions. The development of both will rely on the use and integration of the functions of the total brain which include thinking, feeling, physical/sensing and intuition. By understanding the new data from the brain research, we will be far more able to optimize learning, develop intelligence and nurture giftedness.

Until the 1960s there was a belief that intelligence was fixed and that formal education was designed only to develop skills and dispense information in order to maintain the existing culture. The possibility that schooling could be an effective vehicle for changing the culture and for enabling individuals to become all they could be was, if considered, generally regarded as idealistic and nonsensical. Regarding gifted learners, it was very easy to believe that, if they were "*truly* gifted," they could use their genetic endowment to "get by" and succeed on their own. With intelligence regarded as largely immutable and success as an inevitable accompaniment, those who chose to ignore the special needs of gifted learners could rest comfortably.

The belief that gifted children could succeed on their own was made possible by the dearth of knowledge regarding the brain and how intelligence develops. Such comfort is no longer possible. Old beliefs must be rethought for we now have begun a remarkable inquiry. We are beginning to understand the human brain, how it is organized, how it functions and the impact of the environment on its

Barbara Clark is Professor of Special Education, California State University/Los Angeles, Los Angeles, California. Every summer, Dr. Clark directs The New Age School that she established to provide integrative education for gifted children in the Los Angeles area. Parts of this paper were taken by permission from Clark, B. (1986). *Optimizing Learning: The Integrative Education Model in the Classroom.* Columbus, OH: Charles E. Merrill.

development. Through this understanding we are beginning to see many of our old beliefs challenged. Intelligence, learning and giftedness have new meaning. We now have some clues to how we may optimize learning, develop intelligence, and enhance giftedness.

NEW UNDERSTANDINGS ABOUT INTELLECTUAL DEVELOPMENT

Significant inquiry into the nature of the brain and intelligence began with the work of Rosenzweig (1966) and Krech (1969) in the laboratories on the campus of the University of California at Berkeley. They asked, "Can the brain of mammals be changed by the environment?" Not only did they find that environmental impact was significant, they later found these changes were directly correlated to the levels of intelligence developed in individuals.

From that beginning, years of research have produced significant information about the nature of intelligence. We now know, for example, that learning is reflected in the brain by the exchange of impulses from one neuron to the next, setting up more and more complex chains of neural response patterns. Each of our hundred thousand neurons comes equipped with numerous rather complex sets of extensions called dendrites which, the research has shown, branch and increase in density with appropriate stimulation. The density of the dendritic system has been found to be directly correlated to the intelligence of the individual.

Each neuron in the brain has an axon which carries the impulse from the neuron to the vicinity of the dendrites of other neurons which are prepared to receive the impulse through a biochemical exchange called the synaptic process. Down the axon of one neural cell passes the electrical energy of information. At the closest point to an adjacent dendrite the electrical energy becomes biochemical, allowing neurotransmitter fluid to carry the information across the synaptic gap, a space existing between the axon of one cell and the dendrites of another. As the dendrites pick up the information, the biochemicals are again returned to an electrical impulse and sent to the cell body of the neuron, all within milliseconds. The process is carried on over and over again. It is this process that the research shows to be directly affected by the environment.

The impact of a stimulating environment was found to affect the brain in several ways. There was an increase in dendritic growth, adding to the complexity of the system, and the biochemistry of the

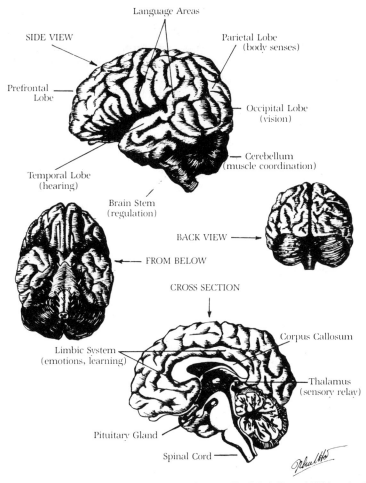

FIGURE 1. The Brain and Its Functions From *Growing Up Gifted*, Second Edition, (p. 18) by B. Clark, 1983, Columbus, Ohio: Charles E. Merrill Publishing Co. Copyright 1983 by Charles E. Merrill. Reprinted by permission.

neurons changed, creating stronger cells. Stimulation also resulted in an increase in myelination of the axon, allowing impulses to be sent with more force, more quickly. And, the stimulating environment produced an increase in neurological cells which support and nurture the brain system. Thus, the critical role of the environment in the development of the brain and its intellectual functions was clearly established.

These early findings were followed up later by researchers like Diamond (1980) and others who specified in more detail the nature of the stimulation and its effects on the brain. With technological capabilities of the Computerized Axial Tomography Scanner (CAT), the Positron Emission Tomography Scanner (PET), the Magnetoencephalogram (MEG) which can map the human brain at work (Zimmerman, 1982), and the Nuclear Magnetic Resonance Scanner (NMR) which provides a window to the interior of the human brain, researchers such as Beckwith (1971), Clarke-Stewart (1973), Yarrow, Ruben, Stein, and Pedersen (1973), Lewis and Rosenblum (1974), White (1975), and Thompson, Berger, and Berry (1980) have demonstrated similar environmental effects on the brains of human subjects. This research base has forced us to reject the comfortable view of the nature of intelligence as static and to conceptualize intelligence as a dynamic process.

Our understanding of intelligence also has been altered regarding when significant growth in the development of intelligence occurs. It was once thought that infants were born with all the intelligence they would ever have available to them; that it was a part of their genetic package. Any deviation which could be observed in the growth of intelligence was thought to be the result of learning, not an actual change in capability or potential. For that reason, it was expected that intelligence would plateau around 18-years-of-age, and at age 45 a slow and steady downward curve toward senility would occur. It is important to note that while this early view of intelligence accurately represented the significant, critical influence of early learning on the development of intellectual potential, it inaccurately limited the possibility of cognitive growth in later years. Buell and Coleman (1981) since have shown that the brain is engaged in growth far into the 80th year of life. Not only is the process not static, it continues throughout our lifespan. The human seems to have unlimited potential for intellectual growth.

The findings of brain researchers now can inform us as to when the environment begins to impact on the intellectual development of the child. With our new ability to follow the development of the fetus, it seems evident that the environment meaningfully interacts with the genetic program of each individual from conception onward. An argument could be made that, even prior to conception, the health of the mother can directly support or limit the growth of the child. Studies from third world countries have shown that, when severely deprived, it will take three generations of both proper nutrition and stimulation to return the human brain to a normal level of intellectual growth.

Verny (1981) reports several interesting events that have been seen to occur during the fetal period and underscore the importance of the environment to the later intellectual development of the child. By 4 months infants in-utero can frown, squint, and grimace; by 5 months they are sensitive to touch and light and reach to sound (e.g., melodies by Vivaldi and Mozart creating a relaxed state while music by Beethoven and Brahms seems to stimulate movement). At 6 months the fetus hears clearly and responds discriminately to mother's speech. During the 6th or 7th month, the attitudes of the mother will be picked up by the child and the mother's attitudes toward the child are regarded by some researchers to be the factor that has the single greatest effect on the unborn's well-being and future welfare.

In addition to data on prenatal development, the bodies of information now available on perinatal and postnatal development certainly add to our knowledge of how we might provide most effectively for optimal intellectual development and support higher levels of intellectual functioning. Perinatal factors that affect the brain in ways that can limit or support intelligence can be seen in the literature on bonding (Kennell & Klaus, 1979) and on the birthing process (Lamaze, 1970; LeBoyer, 1975).

The work of Fantz (1961) identifies the sensitive period for visual complexity as occurring from birth to 2 months. This sensitive period leads to discriminatory viewing and a preference for complex stimuli by 2 months. This was the beginning of the consideration of the infant as a most capable and competent learner. We are now aware that infants orient to sound at birth and already show a preference for their mother's voice (Brazelton & Als, 1979). They also can imitate facial gestures and, within 12 to 21 days, can imitate movement they cannot see themselves perform (Meltzoff & Moore, 1977). By 3 weeks infants will have developed rules and theories, and by 2 months will have established a beginning sense of their locus of control (Lewis, 1972).

At 3 months the rate of language development can be predicted and the infant's ability to laugh at a complex event will predict with good accuracy future intellectual development (Birns & Golden, 1972). By 5 months infants are exhibiting the development of schema and can track objects visually, watching as the objects disappear only to be upset when different objects appear in their stead (Bower, Broughton, & Moore, 1970; Gardner, 1971). All of this is to say that, indeed far earlier than was expected, the child is a thinking, alert, responding being, capable of far more even in infancy than our once simplistic view of intelligence and its development would have indicated.

THE ORGANIZATION OF THE BRAIN

The organization of the brain has been another meaningful area of inquiry. While some researchers believed that the brain was organized into specific areas and others believed that the organization occurred through associative tissue, it now appears that biological integration is built into the system, across hemispheres, throughout the brain, using both specific areas and associative tissue to optimize functions. Such data require that we change our thinking about brain functioning from a partial and separatist perspective to an integrative and holistic approach.

The human brain is organized into three formations or three systems with radically different structures and chemistry. This hierarchy of three-brains-in-one may be called the triune brain (MacLean, 1978). Educationally this organization presents some important considerations. Two of the three brains have no system for verbal communication. Given that it is the integration of total brain function that results in human intelligence, a test that measures primarily verbal communication as its sampling of intelligence may be seen as limited. The three systems are described briefly below.

1. *The reptilian brain*, the oldest brain system, provides autonomic function, the neural pathway for many higher brain centers, motor control, and communication links between the rest of the brain and the cerebellum. It houses the reticular formation which is the physical basis for consciousness and plays a major role in the state of being awake and alert.
2. *The old mammalian brain or limbic system* houses the biochemical centers that are activated by the motions of the learner. This biochemistry enhances or inhibits memory, affects many diverse emotions such as pleasure, joy, anxiety, rage, and sentimentality, and alters the attention span.
3. *The new mammalian brain, the neocortex*, or cerebrum, is where sensory data are processed, decisions are made, and action is initiated. It includes the functions of language and

speech and provides for reception, storage, and retrieval of information. The most recently evolved area of the neocortex, the prefrontal cortex, provides for behaviors associated with planning, insight, empathy, introspection, and other bases for intuitive thought (MacLean, 1978). It is engaged in firming up intention, deciding on action, and regulating a human being's most complex behaviors (Restak, 1979). It is, in fact, the area that energizes and regulates all other parts; it houses the individual's sense of purpose.

From this perspective there are three, somewhat different brains in one: the smallest and oldest, the brain stem; surrounded by the larger, newer brain, the limbic system; and above and around it, the cerebrum or neocortex, the largest brain, consisting of the newest, most sophisticated structures. Under stress this largest, most complex system begins shutting down, turning over more and more functions to the lower, limbic system brain. While rote learning can be continued, higher and more complex learning is inhibited (Hart, 1981, 1983). Creating opportunities for the effective operation of this total triune brain is the responsibility of educators and parents.

Within the last decade a great deal has been published regarding the specialization of the hemispheres of the brain (Bogen, 1977; Gazzaniga, 1978; Pribram, 1978; Levy, 1980). This information has been useful and provided some important insights into the learning process. These very data have been oversimplified, however, and have been used as the basis for many exaggerated claims which are said to result from teaching to the "unused" side of the brain. Such claims are usually partial and often misleading. What will be of importance to those seeking to provide optimal educational experiences is the knowledge that the brain has two major cognitive processes that can be used to support the child's learning, and that the brain is organized to use both specializations in an integrated way regardless of the task to be learned.

While the hemispheres of the brain do show specialization, the entire brain is capable of performing all the activities exhibited by any of its divisions (Pribram, 1978). It would, therefore, be more accurate to speak of one hemisphere leading the other during certain tasks rather than viewing a person as right-brained or left-brained. The goal would be to have available the leadership from the hemisphere whose processes would be most appropriate to the effective solution in any situation. The ability to use the strategies from either hemisphere would be ideal. For most activities, both mental and physical, it is important that we do not overemphasize the separate functions of the hemispheres as the human requires both hemispheres to function in close integration, allowing thereby the understanding of both the computation and the conceptualization of mathematics, the structure and the melody of music, the syntax and the poetry of language. The very complexity of the system joining the two hemispheres, the corpus collosum, biologically prepares the human being for this integration. There are more neural connectors between the hemispheres than to any other part of the body.

AN EXAMINATION OF EDUCATIONAL PRACTICES IN RELATION TO NEW DATA ON BRAIN FUNCTION

Many common educational practices can be seen to be counterindicated by the data provided by recent research on how the human brain functions. First, the brain seems to use at least four major functions: (a) the physical/sensing function of the brain stem in cooperation with other areas of the brain; (b) the emotional or feeling function of the midbrain or limbic area; (c) the cognitive function, both linear/rational and spatial/gestalt, of the cortex; and (d) the intuitive, insightful function of the pre-frontal cortex. Instead of a focus on logical, rational, sequential thought as the center of the educational experience, the new understandings of brain functioning indicate the importance of a focus on the integration of all human brain functions to optimize learning and intellectual growth.

Secondly, one of the first findings from brain research that spoke to the human learning process suggested that when tension and stress reach too high a level, the biochemistry of the brain shuts down higher level functions; the greater the level of tension, the less a person is able to access these functions. Instead, therefore, of using tension-inducing pressure tactics to motivate and control learning behavior, optimal learning conditions require the use of techniques to increase relaxation and reduce tension in the learning setting while releasing natural motivation to learn.

A third concern is the nature of the classroom environment which can no longer be seen simply as a container for the learning process, but now must be regarded as an important tool of learning that contributes to the quality of the educational experience through color, light, and sound. A responsive classroom environment offers stimulation at the level desirable for each individual learner, changing appropriately according to the responses of each. Such an environment is important from the infant's earliest learning experiences. Underscoring the importance of such an environment for optimizing the potential of children, the brain research clearly shows the uniqueness of each child. Each has a unique genetic program which will respond somewhat differently from those of other children to the same environment. If we are, therefore, to provide an optimal learning experience, our fourth concern must be to change our focus from the group to individual learning needs. The same curriculum or experience may not be appropriate for every child; the opportunity to choose from a variety of methods and materials will be needed. Fifth, and closely aligned, we find that our focus must shift from controlling the learning to one of empowering the learner so that all children will be able to meet their needs from diverse available resources. Anything less would be limiting the full development of each child's learning potential.

From the work of such researchers as Luria (1973), Restak (1979), Jeffrey (1980), and Hart (1981, 1983) on the human brain, and Lozanov (1977), Galyean (1977-80, 1978-1981), Wittrock (1980), and Clark (1983) on classroom learning, we can use the following guidelines to improve educational practices:

1. There are four major brain functions, integrative in nature. We can support learning by making it easier to achieve by structuring educational experiences so that children use all four functions simultaneously.
2. Higher levels of brain function are available to be used and developed when tension is reduced. We can teach and use tension reduction techniques.
3. The thinking function is more effective when given novelty, complexity, choice, and alternatives. Instead, therefore, of excessive repetition and simplification in teaching, we should actively provide more complex alternatives and variety.
4. Learners respond positively when challenged by materials and experiences appropriate for their level of cognitive development. Instead of rigid age grouping and inflexible structures, we must provide each child with challenging materials and activities according to his/her developmental readiness.
5. Biochemistry from the midbrain, which is triggered by emotion, can enhance or depress brain function and higher level

thinking. To improve learning we can avoid boredom, same-
ness, fear, anxiety, and threat and intentionally increase novelty, excitement, complexity and pleasure in the educational experiences we provide.
6. The pre-frontal cortex is uniquely human. No other life form
shares this structure of the brain nor its functions. Therefore,
insight, intuition, future planning, and creativity should be encouraged in the learning process.

Appendix 1 provides a more detailed description of the specific
characteristics and educational needs of gifted students that guide
the design of a stimulating environment that is optimally responsive
to each child. Children that are taught in such an environment, according to those guidelines, are: (a) more relaxed, more at ease with
themselves and others; (b) more positive, caring and respectful of
each other and the faculty; (c) more creative, try more unusual solutions and engage in more alternative and higher level cognitive ac-
tivites; (d) more inclined to initiate learning activities, and are more
positive and enthusiastic about their learning; (e) more highly
motivated toward learning; and (f) more independent and responsible (Clark, 1986).

As we alter our educational practices according to the information
we now have about intelligence and optimal learning experiences of
children, we will find those same biological changes occurring that
are being discussed in the brain laboratories throughout the world.
All children will have a better opportunity to actualize their intellectual potential, to expand their capabilities, to become more of
what they are capable of becoming. As these changes occur the child
will change biologically to become a more effective and efficient
learner.

SUMMARY COMMENTS

One message can be heard clearly from the brain data and those
who work in this field, "Use the brain or lose the ability to use it!"
When used, the brain increases in complexity, enriches biochem-
ically, and improves in function. For the first time, we can better
understand how such improved function can result in what we call
giftedness. We can better explain the differences in characteristics
observed between the gifted and the more average learners, dif-

ferences that can now be seen to be biological. From brain research, intelligence can be seen to have biological roots in the changes produced by stimulating learning experiences: (a) an increase in neuroglial cells which results in accelerated synapic activity (Thompson, Berger, Berry, 1980); (b) enriched biochemical changes in the neuron (Rosenzweig, 1966; Krech, 1969); (c) increased use of higher cortical synthesis and pre-frontal lobe activity (MacLean, 1978; Goodman, 1978; Restak, 1979); and (d) more efficient use of associative functions (Martindale, 1975; Lozanov, 1977; Millay, 1981). We affect all of these processes through the degree and kind of stimulation that occurs in the environment we provide our children.

It is now evident that instead of believing that truly gifted children can get by on their own, or that children are gifted only part of the time (i.e., when they behave as gifted), we can now understand that intelligence is dynamic, that it must be used and developed or it will be lost. For that reason, it is critical to provide a responsive, stimulating environment appropriate to all learners' specific needs throughout their lifespace. It is an awesome and exciting challenge for it is possible that human potential is unlimited.

Socioemotional Vulnerabilities of Young Gifted Children

Wendy C. Roedell, PhD

ABSTRACT. Gifted children may experience particular difficulties in growing up because they are different from other children in their area of talent. They are vulnerable to problems resulting from the myths surrounding giftedness, unrealistic expectations for their behavior, pressure to perform, constant criticism or praise, pressures to conform, and difficulties in finding friends. Parents and teachers who understand the social and emotional implications of being gifted can provide an accepting environment and can teach social skills that will help gifted children cope with their differentness.

Gifted individuals are unusually competent in some area of ability or performance, and this unusual quality sets them apart from others. The key to understanding giftedness rests in understanding the unusual, extraordinary nature of gifted behavior, whether it be unusual creativity, outstanding musical talent, superior leadership qualities, or extraordinary intellectual reasoning ability. Being gifted means being different from others with respect to the specific talent area.

Because of the differentness inherent in the nature of giftedness, gifted children face particular difficulties in socioemotional development, these difficulties are not always appreciated by their average peers or even by the adults who love them. The greater the degree of giftedness, and, therefore, the greater the difference from the norm, the more likely it is that a gifted child will experience adjustment problems as a result of coping with the psychological conflict or stress created. Fortunately, however, most gifted children find effective ways of coping with the conflict with minimally nega-

Wendy C. Roedell is Director of the Northwest Gifted Education Center at Educational Service District 121 in Seattle, Washington, and is senior author of the 1980 publication, *Gifted Young Children* (Teachers College Press). This chapter is based in part on work conducted at the Child Development Research Group at the University of Washington, directed by the late Halbert B. Robinson.

tive effects. In study after study, gifted children as a group have demonstrated good social adjustment and healthy, positive self-concepts (Gallagher, 1985; Tannenbaum, 1983; Terman, 1925). Although a child's risk of social maladjustment and unhappiness increases with the degree of giftedness (Hollingworth, 1942; Tannenbaum, 1983, Terman, 1925), it is a mistake to assume that being gifted dooms a child to a life of misery and misfortune. It is also true, however, that a nurturant home environment and a supportive educational experience will enhance the gifted child's total development. Understanding possible areas of emotional vulnerability unique to gifted children in particular can help adults guide the development of enhanced self-awareness and fulfilling interpersonal relationships.

VULNERABILITY CREATED BY MYTHS AND MISINFORMATION ABOUT GIFTEDNESS

Old myths that still prevail regarding giftedness range from the more positive though erroneous expectation—"the gifted can make it on their own because they are superior in every way"—to the very negative and potentially damaging expectancy that "gifted children tend to be maladjusted misfits." Both types of myths burden children who have been identified as gifted with inaccurate, stereotyped expectations of what a gifted child should be, that is, stereotypes that make them vulnerable to social and emotional difficulties.

These myths also do a great deal to hinder identification. One of the most pressing problems facing a young gifted child is the possibility that his or her giftedness will be denied. Parents have frequently confided to me that they are certain their child cannot be gifted because on a checklist of characteristics of gifted chldren they found one or two their child did not possess. Teachers' misconceptions of giftedness can lead to error in referrals for identification. After describing a second grader's exceptional creative writing abilities and advanced reasoning skills, one teacher still maintained firmly that the child could not be gifted because "she doesn't march to a different drummer."

The truth is that the personalities and individual characteristics of gifted children vary tremendously. Thomas and Chess (1977) found no relationship between IQ and temperament characteristics of children in their longitudinal study of temperament development.

Parents of intellectually gifted children in Seattle who responded to the Thomas and Chess Temperament questionnaire reported wide variation in their children's temperament characteristics (Roedell, Jackson, & Robinson, 1980). Even in studies where particular temperaments or learning styles are shown to be characteristic of a group of gifted students (Dunn & Price, 1980), not every child in the study exhibits the same set of characteristics. Yet, we persist in denying giftedness on the basis of mythical characteristics while ignoring real evidence of advanced cognitive ability.

Part of the problem lies in the mystique surrounding the identification process. Many of us are convinced that when we are identifying gifted children, we are actually trying to predict which children are going to become the "leaders of tomorrow." We are told that giftedness in children represents potential, and that true giftedness resides in the adult who is exceptionally productive in ways highly valued by society (Tannenbaum, 1983). Small wonder, then, that few educators try to identify gifted children during the preschool or primary years. How could it be possible to predict which of a group of wiggly 4-year-olds is going to win a Nobel prize some day? Many primary teachers avoid any attempt at identifying gifted children, fearful that in 20 or 30 years, the country's next Einstein will come back to visit with the accusation of not being identified for the gifted program at age 6. Better to identify no one than to make a blunder of this magnitude. This crystal ball approach to identification makes most educators extremely uncomfortable, and rightly so.

Arguments ensue over whether a child is "truly gifted" or "just precocious or mature." If a 4-year-old is reading, scoring well in IQ tests, and engaging in debates about the meaning of justice, adults may question whether he/she is a "truly" gifted chld, or just one whose parents have spent a lot of time and energy providing stimulating interaction. By "truly gifted" we usually mean a child that will grow up to contribute significantly to society. Meanwhile, as educators debate, the 4-year-old may languish until third or fourth grade before someone tries to provide an educational experience that challenges his or her thinking and builds upon advanced academic skills to create a genuine sense of self-worth and potential for rewarding high achievement.

A more fruitful approach to the identificaton process takes a comprehensive view of the child's patterns of strengths and weaknesses, and makes sound educational decisions based on what we know about that child's immediate needs. It really doesn't matter what that child will do in 20 years. What does matter is what the child needs right now. Acknowledgement and support for the development of a child's specific advanced abilities is the first major step toward assuring a positive developmental path and reducing conditions that make the child vulnerable to inappropriate expectations.

PEAKS AND VALLEYS:
THE IMPLICATIONS OF UNEVEN DEVELOPMENT

A second source of socioemotional vulnerability for young gifted children is related to patterns of uneven development and adult expectations of overall accelerated development. Anyone who has spent some time with a young gifted child has probably been struck by the unsettling combination of mature skill development in some areas coupled with less advanced, although age appropriate, behavior in others. It is disconcerting to be engaged in a philosophical discussion about the meaning of friendship with an articulate 5-year-old who five minutes later becomes embroiled in a physical confrontation with a friend over the possession of a toy truck. The adult's immediate reaction is to cry, "You know better than that!," thinking back to the ideas expressed earlier during their conversation. While the child may know better intellectually, the translation of knowledge into behavior may still be at an immature 5-year-old level (Roedell, 1985).

Adults are frequently misled by a child's specific advanced abilities into expecting equal advancement in all areas on all occasions. Expectations for consistent high-level performance unrelated to a child's actual pattern of strengths and weaknesses in specific abilities may burden the young child with feelings of inadequacy because those expectations cannot be fulfilled. In fact, one of the most common complaints listed by gifted children from age 7 through 18 has been summarized by Galbraith (1985) as "Parents, teachers, and friends expect us to do our best and be perfect all the time." This source of vulnerability is illustrated by the parent who expressed concern to me because her daughter, an "A" student and accomplished musician, was not "exerting herself" to be first on the community swimming team. "If she would only try," the parent explained, "she could be the best." The parent failed to recognize that, even if the child's ability to perform in swimming was equal to the parent's ambition, her motivation to "be the best" in that area was not equal to her motivation in other areas of endeavor.

Adults need to remember that, in spite of multiple talents, children must make selective decisions about where to invest their time and energy. No one can be the best at everything, even if the talent exists; there simply isn't enough time. Uneven development in talent areas is bound to occur, as much because of differential motivation and opportunity as because of differential talents. Constant criticism over specific performance areas where the child is not "the best" can damage the child's general feelings of competence and self-worth. Adults must guard against developing unrealistic high expectations that foster low self-esteem in their children.

In contrast, sometimes adults are misled by a child's uneven development into forming expectations for performance that are too low. A first grade teacher may assume, for example, that because a child's handwriting is sloppy, and his or her work isn't turned in neatly, that the child's thinking ability is average or below. The underestimation of ability by teachers can have a damaging effect on bright children. Pringle (1970), for example, found that many of the gifted children brought to a clinic for maladjustment problems had teachers who underestimated their ability and did not encourage them. In a study of first and second grade children, Sutherland and Goldschmidt (1974) found that negative teacher expectations can actually have a detrimental effect on the intellectual development of bright children.

Young children also are vulnerable because of their tendency to hold expectations for their own performance that are just as unrealistic as some adult expectations; they too can fail to accept the unevenness of their development. Young gifted children can become extremely frustrated when their limited fine motor skills, for example, prevent the completion of the marvelous project conceptualized by their advanced intellect. Adult understanding and sensitive guidance can help children develop a problem-solving approach to handling such frustrating situations (Abroms, 1983; Roedell, 1985; Whitmore, 1980).

Another side-effect of uneven development can be the exposure to highly complex, emotionally-charged information that the child may not be mature enough to understand. The parent of an intellectually advanced 4-year-old described how he came upon his daughter looking terrified as she read the Bible. When he inquired about her concern, she replied, "I'm reading the Book of Revelations, and it's really scary!'' Young children who read the newspapers or watch the television news without a context for understanding global problems may need some help interpreting the events described. Parent explanations and comments concerning television events can have a positive influence on children's responses (e.g., Collins, Sobel, & Westby, 1981), and can help an advanced child sort out the complexities of potentially misunderstood material.

THE PRESSURE TRAP

Most parents and teachers want very much to provide an optimum environment that will foster the full development of children's potential. Some adults are so overwhelmed by the concept of giftedness, however, that they put unceasing pressure on themselves and on their children not to waste a moment that might be devoted to talent development. Their motivation for the child's high achievement creates another source of vulnerability for the gifted youngster. Parents, in particular, may become extremely anxious when informed that their child is gifted, worrying that they might not do the right thing. In talking with a group of parents of gifted children, I was asked a question by one parent who described a child unmotivated to do academic tasks, who refused to sit down with paper and pencil and work on reading and writing skills. "How might this child be motivated?" asked the parent. I replied, "How old is your child?" The answer: "Three." This type of unrealistic expectation for the behavior of a 3-year-old stems from genuine parental concern over the need to develop the child's abilities, coupled with ignorance about how young children learn.

When I was director of the Child Development Preschool for Gifted Children at the University of Washington, parents frequently complained about a lack of rigor in the curriculum. For example, one parent wanted homework assigned to the 4-year-olds. Other parents were hard to convince that exploration of manipulative materials and work with Cuisenaire rods were really developing their children's understanding of mathematics; they wanted to see workbook sheets coming home with numbers written on them.

Although preschool-age gifted children may have intellectual abilities more similar to the thinking of children two or three years older, they retain the young child's need to learn through active exploration and manipulation of concrete materials. The task of their teacher is to translate advanced concepts into an appropriate frame-work of early childhood educational experiences so that gifted young children can satisfy their intellectual curiosity without being stifled by rigid teaching methods. Similarly, teachers need to help parents understand the learning needs of young children. Too often educators dismiss a concerned parent's complaints as simply the whining of a "pushy parent." Parents need sympathetic understanding of their concerns as well as information about how their children will learn best.

An additional parental concern centers on the fact that sometimes gifted children's skills may not develop in a smooth progression, but rather may evolve in a series of spurts interspersed with plateaux. A child might enter preschool knowing all letters and letter sounds, and leave at the end of the year still not knowing how to read, in spite of numerous opportunities to interact with the written word. At some point in that same child's development he/she may, in a matter of weeks, become a fluent reader. The development of reading skills, however, may not progress at an even rate. Parents, and even teachers, may become concerned if a child who seems "ready" to read does not begin at the expected time, even though the child is still very young. Adults need to relax a bit, and observe carefully just how many things the child may be learning that are equally as important as specific academic skills, with the assurance that those skills will emerge with time. Increased pressure will be more likely to delay than to accelerate that learning.

Parents do have an important role to play in arranging stimulating experiences that encourage talent development (Bloom, 1982). There is a fine line, however, between responding appropriately to a child's interest and pushing a learning experience that an adult has determined is important. Careful observation of children's interests and activities can help parents and teachers design learning environments that offer a wide range of stimulating choices without pressure to excel in any one area.

THE TRAP OF CONSTANT PRAISE

Some parents are so delighted with the exploits of their gifted child that they greet every little accomplishment with lavish praise. Overpraising can have a number of negative effects that are sources of psychological vulnerability. One consequence is skepticism on the part of the child. One father described how his 4-year-old daughter ran up to him at a time he was busy working to show him a drawing. "Oh, that's beautiful," he commented without paying much attention. He then heard his daughter explain to her friend, "See, I told you he likes scribbles! I don't know why, but he does." Obviously, she had been testing his reaction. When children are exposed too frequently to global evaluations, whether in the form of comments or grades with no feedback, they quickly begin to discount the meaning. An aspiring writer, age 8, commented, "They keep giving me A's when I know that I can do better."

Constant praise also can engender the suspicion that parents or teachers are constantly evaluating the child, and that if the child ever falls short, love will be withdrawn. The fear that a parent only loves a child because of the child's accomplishments can be a real problem for gifted children. Such children may grow up to feel like imposters, both during their school years and in their adult lives: they begin to believe they have fooled others into thinking they are smart or talented when, in reality, they "know" they are nowhere nearly as brilliant as others believe. Fear of being unmasked can drive talented individuals to lead unhappy lives full of tension and worry (Chance, 1985; Harvey & Katz, 1985). Also, children need to accept their weaknesses, to learn from their mistakes, and to become comfortable with constructive criticism and errors as a necessary part of appropriately challenging learning. If success is too easily attained and praise is too lavish, the child can develop inappropriately low expectations just as too much criticism and inappropriately difficult tasks can convey unattainable high expectations and develop feelings of inadequacy in the child.

As with the responsiveness versus pressure issue discussed above, adults have another tightrope to walk regarding the fine line between praise and encouragement. There is a subtle but important difference between looking at a child's drawing and saying, "That's great," and saying, "That's an interesting use of the color blue. The way you put those wavy lines across the middle makes me feel peaceful. You've really been working hard on this picture." The first statement may encourage a belief that everything is either good or bad, and may become internalized as a critical inner voice, constantly evaluating everything the child does. The second approach conveys interest and appreciation, and leaves the door open to ongoing communication where the child and the adult might share ideas about the work.

THE TRAP OF CONFORMITY

Young children are extremely social beings which makes them vulnerable to the psychological trap of social conformity. Much of their learning takes place through observations of how others behave. If a highly gifted child spends all of his or her time in the company of same-age children of average mental ability, that child may try to fit in by hiding advanced intellectual abilities and attempting to act "average" (Whitmore, 1980). When confronted by a parent concerned about the school experience of her highly gifted 5-year-old, one principal commented, "Just put her in kindergarten, and soon she'll be just like everyone else." The sad truth is, it happens. Parents and teachers must guide young gifted children in finding ways to "fit in" socially without hiding their talents or denying their individuality. The valuing of individuality and diversity should be genuinely affirmed at home and school.

The problem may be particularly difficult for girls (Silverman, in press), and can happen even in schools sensitive to the needs of the gifted. One first grade teacher in a gifted program related how the school first identified a young girl who had spent an unremarkable kindergarten year, fitting in well with all the other children. In first grade, her class went to the library where she attempted to check out a fairly advanced book. The librarian gently steered her to the picture book section, commenting that she wouldn't be able to read the book she had chosen. The first indication to anyone at the school that the child was a fluent reader occurred when the mother sent a note to the school saying that her daughter had been reading since age 3 and requested that the school allow her use of the library. At that point, of course, teachers looked a bit closer and found that the child was qualified for the gifted program.

Stories such as this abound among educators and parents who have dealt with the gifted (Whitmore, 1980). There are two lessons to be learned here. The first lesson is that no matter how supportive the school environment, parents of unusual children need to alert the school personnel to their child's special abilities. For example, it is never a good idea to wait for two years to inform teachers that they have neglected to notice early reading ability. Since children can be excellent at hiding their skills, teachers need help in recognizing and encouraging the expression of children's special capabilities. The second lesson is that teachers need to welcome parental discussion of gifted children's talents without becoming defensive.

Too frequently parents and teachers end up in a noncommunicative standoff. The parent wants to be sure the teacher knows about the child's abilities, and begins to tell the teacher all the wonderful things the child can do. Defensively, the teacher thinks that the parent has an unrealistic view of the child, and proceeds to explain all of the child's flaws. The parent, thinking that the teacher has overlooked the child's real strengths, continues to explain while the teacher continues to describe how the child's handwriting, social skills, and perhaps particular academic abilities are not up to par. The teacher may not have seen the extent of the child's real abilities in the classroom. Parents, on the other hand, may not have a good understanding of how their child responds in a group learning situation. Both parent and teacher have a great deal to learn from each other, and this learning can only benefit the child.

FINDING FRIENDS

"I sent my daughter to preschool to learn to get along with other 3-year-olds, and all she does is sit in the corner and read," complained a parent. When asked if her daughter ever played with other children, she replied, "Of course. She loves to play checkers and Monopoly with her older sister's friends." These are hardly interests to be shared with other 3-year-olds.

Although the research literature suggests that gifted children tend to be a popular group (Gallagher, 1985; Tannebaum, 1983), many individuals are not classified as popular with their peers and, furthermore, report difficulty finding "true friends." Intellectually gifted young children are particularly vulnerable to feelings of social isolation and/or discomfort and conflict. A highly gifted child particularly is apt to have a limited selection of children from which to develop friendships. Janos, Marwood, and Robinson (1985), for example, found that 8-year-old children with extremely high IQs were more likely than moderately high IQ children to have friends who were older than themselves. Also, they were more likely to report that they did not have enough friends and that being smart made it harder for them to make friends. This fits with Hollingworth's (1942) finding that highly gifted children tend to have older, and fewer, friends, and with O'Shea's (1960) finding that highly gifted children often form friendships with others of similar mental age.

One explanation for this phenomenon could be the possibility that friends are more likely to be found among intellectual peers, based on developmental characteristics rather than chronological age. If by peers we mean others with whom we can intereact at an equal level around issues of common interest (Lewis, Young, Brooks, & Michelson, 1975), then the differences in ability between gifted children and average agemates may make friendship formation unavoidably difficult. In fact, Janos et al. (1985) found that gifted children who perceived themselves as different from others were more likely to have difficulties in social adjustment.

Parents and teachers wishing to help a gifted child form friendships might first attempt to group the child with others who have similar interests and skill levels in certain areas. Children with uneven development may have several sets of developmental peers, depending on the activity and situation. One group might provide peers when riding tricycles, for example, while a different group might be peers when reading and discussing books. Discussions illustrating what children have in common can enhance the possibilities of friendship formation. A gifted child who wishes to play with a classmate might have more success choosing an activity both will enjoy, such as basketball, rather than an activity that is too advanced for the potential friend, such as chess.

FOSTERING POSITIVE SOCIAL AND EMOTIONAL GROWTH

When parents and teachers understand the implications of the differentness inherent in being gifted, they can create conditions that will support the child's positive social and emotional growth. The first step is to realize the inextricable link between social and cognitive development. Some educators reason that there is no need to provide programs for young gifted children because the goal of early childhood education is socialization. A major component of socialization, however, involves a child's feeling that he or she is accepted by others, teachers and children alike. If the teacher does not validate a gifted child's abilities and intellectual interests by including them in the ongoing curriculum, the child begins to wonder about acceptance from the teacher. If the child also makes the discovery that communication with classmates is difficult and that others do not share his/her vocabulary, skills, or interests, peer interactions may be limited and unsatisfactory. We cannot ignore the gifted child's need for intellectual stimulation and expect social development to flourish (Whitmore, 1980).

The best early childhood education program will provide an optimal match between the child's skills and interests and the qualities of the learning situation, with balanced opportunities for rewarding challenge in areas of strength as well as successful development of skills in areas of weakness (Roedell et al., 1980). Included in the planned curriculum will be an organized program to guide the development of a realistic, positive self-concept and increased interpersonal skills (Roedell, 1985).

Social skills can be enhanced informally through teacher modeling and encouragement as well as formally through planned lessons. Teachers can adapt training programs that focus on social problem-solving skills (Spivack & Shure, 1974; Elardo & Cooper, 1977) to help gifted children increase their repertoire of interaction strategies (Abroms, 1983; Roedell, 1985). Some research indicates that gifted young children are quite capable of reasoning at high levels about social situations, but that they have difficulty translating their ideas into action (Abroms, 1983; Roedell, 1985). If this is the case, programmatic attempts to help children practice their ideas through role playing or puppetry may be particularly important.

CONCLUSION

Young gifted children are an eager, friendly, curious, and altogether delightful group of individuals. Like all young children, they face some difficulties in growing up. Because they are gifted, and therefore different from many of the children around them, they have some unique areas of vulnerability, and may be subject to some unique pressures. Expectations for their performance may be unrealistically high or possibly too low. Concerned parents and teachers may push inappropriate educational experiences out of a desire to maximize the development of potential. Feelings of inadequacy or of being an "imposter" can result from overdoses of praise or criticism. Pressure to conform can trigger self-consciousness about advanced skills, and it may be difficult to find a real friend to share ideas and enthusiasms.

Most gifted children, however, adjust well, particularly if they have the emotional support and guidance of understanding adults.

Discussions aimed at helping children understand and appreciate the differences among people, while also learning about the commonalities they share with other children, can enhance peer relationships and individual self-concepts. Guidance in developing effective interpersonal skills can help children cope with situations where they may be the youngest in a group of older children who offer intellectual stimulation, or the most advanced in a group of average agemates. Social guidance is most effective when offered in a context that also provides opportunities for enhancement of the gifted child's advanced abilities.

PART II:
RECOGNIZING INTELLECTUAL GIFTEDNESS IN YOUNG CHILDREN

Introduction

As long as giftedness was defined only as exceptionally high achievement, particularly on standardized tests of intellectual ability, there was a belief that gifted children could not be reliably identified until the middle elementary school years (typically grades 3 and 4). As the field of Special Education created a concern for early recognition of "high risk" children, and for the provision of appropriate intervention to minimize negative effects of the handicapping condition and to optimally develop the child's potential abilities, attention was directed in some school systems to comparable procedures for identifying young gifted children. Today, however, there are relatively few systems committed to identifying and serving gifted children upon entry to school. Thus, for many gifted children, school does not provide the desirable stimulation and guidance afforded by appropriate educational programming during the last phase of the critical early years that so profoundly shape the motivation, attitudes, and behavior of children.

The principal issues raised regarding methods of identifying young gifted children are: (a) At what age can giftedness be reliably assessed? (b) What are reliable indicators or characteristics of intellectual giftedness? (c) What are appropriate tests of intellectual ability and proper use of test scores? (d) To what extent can parents and teachers be reliable sources of information in the identification process? The authors contributing to this publication believe that early recognition of gifted characteristics by parents and/or teachers is possible and necessary so that optimal conditions for the full development of exceptional cognitive abilities can be provided. We believe that specific characteristics of how the child processes information, thinks and learns, can provide reliable evidence of cognitive giftedness (i.e., superior abilities to assimilate, organize for storage, and retrieve information for use in further learning or problem solving). Keen observers of young children, in stimulating and relatively unstructured environments, most commonly recognize intellectual giftedness in a young child's superior memory, use of language, analytical and creative problem-solving skills, perception of relationships, manipulation of abstract symbols and ideas, higher level questioning and critical thinking. Young gifted children also often distinguish themselves by manifesting exceptional drives to be creative, self-expressive, independent in thought, and to know, understand, and master skills.

Tests are valuable as a means of gaining a more objective, controlled sample of a child's abilities. If testing conditions are good (i.e., the child responds well to the examiner and is motivated to do well, the examiner is skilled in establishing rapport with children and in observing behavior for significant clues during testing, and the content of the test is an accurate sample of what the child is capable of doing in relation to the question being asked by the user of the results) then test scores provide an efficient way to evaluate a child's abilities. To the extent that those conditions do not exist, however, the test scores obtained will be inaccurate indicators. If high scores suggesting superior cognitive abilities are obtained, one can assume confidently that the child is capable of high academic achievement. The reverse, however, is *not* true: low scores do not necessarily provide reliable evidence that the child does not possess exceptional intellectual abilities, and the low score should not be used to exclude a child from appropriate programming for gifted children when other indicators (i.e., observations) suggest the child would benefit from them.

The authors contributing articles to this section are distinguished by their history of involvement with the identification issues and their success in addressing them with special subpopulations that tend to be underidentified and underserved by gifted programs, though one can expect an equal percentage of each population to qualify as gifted. Merle Karnes, an international leader in identification and intervention with preschool handicapped as well as gifted children, and her colleague, Lawrence Johnson, report their findings based on research conducted in the University of Illinois preschool projects. They will describe assessment techniques they have found effective for identifying gifted children in both handicapped and nonhandicapped preschool populations. Virginia Ehrlich of Teachers College of Columbia University will discuss problems encountered in identifying gifted children, drawing on experiences with the very varied populations of New York City, particularly with reference to economically disadvantaged, culturally different, and minority groups. She will cite examples and successful procedures used to identify preschool/primary gifted children for participation in what has become an internationally recognized model for early childhood education of the gifted, the Astor Program of New York City.

Identification and Assessment of Gifted/Talented Handicapped and Nonhandicapped Children in Early Childhood

Merle B. Karnes, EdD
Lawrence J. Johnson, PhD

ABSTRACT. This article addresses issues related to the identification and assessment of young handicapped and nonhandicapped gifted children. Identification methods that include both formal and informal sources of data are described. Procedures to evalute the quality of identification and assessment plans are discussed. State guidelines regulating the identification of gifted children are presented and critiqued. Finally, two programs in progress at the University of Illinois, one for young gifted/talented handicapped children and the other for young nonhandicapped gifted/talented, are presented as illustrative of effective procedures for identifying and programming for the young gifted/talented population.

Until very recently, identification and programming for the gifted/talented have focused on nonhandicapped children nine years of age and older. In the late seventies, Jenkins (1979) conducted a study to determine the extent of programming for preschool and primary-age gifted children nationwide. Her survey revealed only 113 programs at these levels. Only 20 were at the kindergarten level, and only 5 were below kindergarten. In a more recent survey, Karnes, Shwedel, and Linnemeyer (1982) were particularly concerned about the lack of identification and programming at the preschool level. They contacted state departments to determine whether

Merle B. Karnes is a Professor of Special Education and of Elementary and Early Childhood Education at the University of Illinois, Urbana-Champaign; Director of a number of Federally, State and/or locally supported programs for handicapped and for gifted preschool children; and Editor of the journal for the Early Childhood Education Division of the Council for Exceptional Children. Lawrence J. Johnson is Assistant Professor of Special Education at the University of Illinois, Urbana-Champaign, and serves as principal evaluator on the numerous projects directed by Dr. Karnes.

there had been any progress in identification and programming below age 5. The survey provided locations of programs serving 3- and 4-year-olds, but a follow-up of these sites revealed few had organized ongoing programs. One reason for this state of affairs is that few states have legislation that allows public schools to use public funds to program for the gifted and talented below age 5. Also, private programs for preschool-age gifted children may not have been known to state personnel.

A review of model programs for young gifted children funded by the Federal government identified only four: one for nonhandicapped gifted at the University of Washington, funded partially by the former Federal Office of the Gifted, and three for the gifted/talented handicapped funded by the Bureau of Education for the Handicapped, now called the Office of Special Education Programs —one at the Child Development Association, Coeur D'Alene, Idaho, also funded partially by the former Office of the Gifted; another in the Chapel Hill Public Schools; and the third at the University of Illinois. Only two of these programs are still in operation: one at the University of Washington and the one at the University of Illinois. Both are funded now from sources other than the Federal government.

There are several reasons why identification plans do not focus on young children. First, identification and programming for the gifted and talented is generally postponed until children are nine years of age, the main reason being that it is easier to identify the functionally gifted child at that time. Children 9 and older tend to be more stable in their performance than younger children; moreover, the older the child, the greater the number of standardized instruments available to assist in identification. Secondly, it is generally not until gifted children reach fourth grade that their parents begin voicing concern about appropriate programming to school authorities. Parents have not been so assertive in demanding programs for their young gifted children (Karnes, Shwedel, & Kemp, 1985). It follows that parental pressure often results in a more organized program for identification and programming for older children who are gifted and talented. Thirdly, specialists in gifted education who advocate for the gifted, and are responsible for developing programs and conducting inservice training for teachers, are usually not trained to work with the young gifted child nor have they gained experience working with them during their professional training. They tend accordingly to advocate for programs starting at the upper elementary school level.

Given that young gifted children often go unidentified and under-served, the young gifted child with a handicap is even more likely to be overlooked. The training of special educators of the handicapped usually does not include understanding gifted children and programming for them. Instead, special educators tend to fixate on children's handicaps and fail to identify and program for strengths. On the other hand, gifted educators seldom have training that would help them understand handicapping conditions and how to identify the gifted and talented among the handicapped.

The strengths of a small percentage of the handicapped, if fully developed, may place them in the category of the gifted and talented. Research on young disadvantaged and handicapped children endorses the belief that the earlier we identify a child's weaknesses and program to alleviate or compensate for problems interfering with full development, the better the child's chance of actualizing his or her potential (The Consortium for Longitudinal Studies, 1983; Karnes, Shwedel, Lewis, Ratts, & Esry, 1981; Kirk, 1958; Lazar & Darlington, 1979; Schweinhart & Weikart, 1980). While longitudinal research on the young gifted talented child is limited, especially studies designed with control or comparison groups, it stands to reason that if early identification and intervention for the disadvantaged and handicapped yield large dividends, positive results are likewise to be expected if the gifted and talented receive appropriate programming at an early age. "Motivation to learn, persistence at task, interpersonal skills, fundamental values, standards of quality, and self-concept are all strongly influenced by significant adults in the child's early years." On the other hand, "by the time the child turns six, the entrenchment of attitudes and behaviors makes them difficult to modify" (Karnes, et al., 1985, p. 204).

Essential to providing services for young gifted/talented children are appropriate identification and assessment methods, which the present article addresses under four headings: (a) Identification Methods: Formal and Informal; (b) Evaluation of Screening, Identification, and Assessment Methods; (c) State Guidelines Influencing Identification Methods; (d) Implementation of Identification and Assessment Procedures at the University of Illinois.

IDENTIFICATION METHODS: FORMAL AND INFORMAL

While it may be difficult to identify the gifted/talented child at a very early age, we know far more about this process than we are practicing at present. There is little justification, of course, for identifying and labeling a child as gifted/talented unless there is a viable plan for programming for that child. Bagnato and Neisworth (1979, 1980) stress the importance of the link between assessment and programming for handicapped children, and the same holds true for gifted and talented children. But even when there is a commitment among educators and parents that early identification and programming are important, a lack of financial backing often inhibits initiating and sustaining a program. Fees from parents are currently the main source of funds for programs for gifted/talented children under 5 years of age. If parents do not have the financial resources to pay fees, their gifted children may not receive an appropriate program.

In developing an identification plan it is important to determine the nature of the program. If the emphasis is on nurturing talent in the visual and performing arts, it will hardly do to use a measure of intellectual functioning as the sole criterion in identification. Just as obviously, if the main goal is to enhance cognitive/language functioning, a measure of musical talent will not identify the best candidates. In the section on the identification of gifted/talented among the states, it will be noted that a multi-faceted approach is customarily used, and rightly so.

Formal Sources of Data

Only a limited number of standardized tests can be used to identify the young gifted child. None were developed primarily for this population. Over the years, the most popular test of intellectual functioning has been the Stanford-Binet Intelligence Scale, Form L-M. Since Terman and Odom (1959) found that giftedness as measured by "the Binet" was highly correlated with giftedness in adulthood, it is understandable that gifted educators have had so much confidence in this instrument. At one time, an IQ score was the only criterion used in most programs to determine eligibility for inclusion. No longer is the IQ score considered to be sufficient in determining the presence of giftedness or talent.

Currently the most reliable instruments available are standardized intelligence and achievement tests. While considerable work has been done in developing creativity tests, their reliability is lower. Recently tests of critical thinking have been developed, and efforts have begun toward constructing tests to assess task persistence, growth in risk-taking, and changes in self-concept. These instruments, like the creativity tests, so far do not seem to provide highly reliable information.

Examples of standardized tests of aptitude and achievement that have been used in some programs to identify and/or to assess young gifted/talented children are shown in Appendix 2.

In recent years, criterion-referenced measures have been used primarily at the preschool level with handicapped children. Such instruments are designed to determine the child's mastery of specific skills and are concerned with group standards. Usually, the items are developmentally sequenced. Performance may or may not be reported in age scores. The commercially available instruments are generally for children up to the age of 6 and are thus inappropriate, since gifted children of these chronological ages may well reach the ceiling. The Brigance tests are a good example of such instruments. While Brigance instruments go beyond the 6-year level, the developer does not claim that they are valuable for assessing non-handicapped gifted children. At the University of Illinois, an initial effort has been made to develop a criterion-referenced test in six areas of talent which are included in the Federal definition (Marland, 1972): intellectual, academic, creative, performing arts (music and art), social and emotional (leadership), and psycho-motor.

Informal Sources of Data

In the past, we often relied too heavily on formal sources of data. While data from standardized and criterion-referenced tests are valuable, it must be remembered that any test taps only a small sampling of the child's abilities. Identification should seek a broader spectrum of information and include other, less formal sources of information. Qualitative data, such as the ability to solve problems, creative and productive thinking skills, creative use of words, leadership skills, skills in the visual and performing arts, and intellectual interests, are best assessed by informal techniques (Karnes, Shwedel, & Linnemeyer, 1982). Among informal sources are anecdotal records, teacher nominations, parent nominations, peer nominations, community nominations, and products from the child.

Anecdotal Records

Keeping in mind the characteristics of gifted/talented children, anecdotal records based on ongoing classroom activities can be very helpful in determining whether a child is talented in certain areas. The skilled teacher can learn a great deal about a child's level of functioning in the various facets of development through careful observation using guidelines that focus on specific behaviors indicative of the child's gifts and talents. Observation also can determine the style of a child's learning. Parents, volunteers, and paraprofessionals can be trained to observe certain types of behavior and to write anecdotal records to share with professionals.

Teacher Nominations

Teachers are an excellent source of information. They have direct contact with children over an extended time and are in a position to compare one child's performance with that of others the same age; thus, they have a yardstick by which to measure outstanding performance against average performance. Karnes and Associates (1978) have developed checklists of characteristics of young gifted/ talented children. Renzulli and Hartman (1971) developed a set of 10 checklists for teachers or parents that have been found to be very useful in identifying gifted/talented students of any age.

There is little research on the effectiveness of nominations from teachers of young children. All data on teacher nominations suggest that even teachers of older students generally do a poor job of nominating them without guidance as to the characteristics of gifted children (Barbe, 1964; Pegnato & Birch, 1959). Fortunately, it also appears that the relative effectiveness of teacher nominations can be enhanced by training (Borland, 1979; Gear, 1978; Roedell, Jackson, & Robinson, 1980).

Parent Nominations

Parents are in the best position to observe the child in a wide range of situations. They see, for instance, how the child interacts with adults and with children, how the child functions in familiar and unfamiliar surroundings, and how the child approaches difficult situations.

Research indicates, in general, that parents are fairly realistic about their children's abilities and that their nominations are an efficient tool for identifying gifted children (Roedell et al., 1980). Some have suggested that parents are the best source for identifying young preschool children (Hagen, 1980). There appear, however, to be differences in the abilities of parents from different socioeconomic groups to make appropriate nominations. Three studies have found that parents from lower socioeconomic backgrounds were more likely to recognize their child as gifted than were parents from upper socioeconomic backgrounds (Cheyney, 1962; Ciha, Harris, Hoffman, & Potter, 1974; Roedell et al., 1980). As Roedell et al. suggest, well-educated parents from homogeneous middle- and upper-income communities tend to be unrealitsically stringent in their standards for superior ability. Furthermore, their lack of a realistic frame of reference as to "typical" behavior in a particular age group may prevent them from making accurate judgments of giftedness. It seems reasonable that parents, like teachers, could benefit from training in recognizing the characteristics of gifted children, prior to participating in an identification plan.

Peer Nominations

An often overlooked source of information is peers, a particularly good source when one is interested in identifying children with outstanding leadership abilities or special talents in areas like music or art. Young children are not good sources, however, when one is interested in superior academic or intellectual abilities (Hagen, 1980). It seems that young children are less sensitive to these differences. Most children know who the leaders of the classroom are and can identify those with outstanding artistic and musical talents, but the accuracy of this information decreases with very young children. Hagen (1980) has asserted that very young children do not understand the task of judging their peers. Therefore, peer nominations are probably more suited to children in the primary grades and older.

Community Nominations

Like peer nominations, nominations from the broader community are often overlooked. Some children participate in organized programs outside the school, programs covering a range of topics such as art, music, computer literacy, and science. Although there is great variation in the intensity and type of program, the people conducting them may provide valuable information about the child's performance in a specific area not included in the school experience.

Another source is family physicians or pediatricians, who sometimes have long histories working with children in their preschool years. As Shwedel and Stoneburner (1983) point out, properly guided physicians are in an ideal position to make the earliest referrals on children whom they perceive as "fast developers" or potentially gifted.

Products From the Child

Products the child has created can be an extremely important source of information. Samples of writing, painting, and sculpture can provide us with a sense of the child's technical skill in a specific area and can be invaluable if we are trying to judge the child's creativity or originality in art. Another important means of determining creative ability in verbal expression is to critique samples of writing—original stories, poetry, accounts of happenings. It is important that an effort be made to collect samples of the child's products in the particular talent area for which a program is being offered.

EVALUATION OF SCREENING, IDENTIFICATION, AND ASSESSMENT METHODS

Choosing appropriate methods to identify and assess gifted children is one of the most perplexing problems facing today's educators. In part, this difficulty stems from the nature of giftedness. An individual's degree of giftedness is not something that can be directly measured like height or weight. Rather, giftedness must be inferred from indirect data. The problem, therefore, is to identify a set of appropriate sources of data that are accurate indicators of giftedness. When developing procedures to identify and assess giftedness and talent, there are at least four important considerations: validity, reliability, harmony, and practicality.

Validity

Perhaps the most important consideration for an identification and assessment plan is the validity of information obtained. Validity can be thought of as the degree to which a test or procedure provides information relevant to the decision to be made. In other words, do the tests or procedures used in the identification plan measure what they purport to measure?

Several steps should be taken to help ensure the development of a valid identification and assessment plan. First, it is imperative that multiple sources of information be used. Using multiple sources of information maximizes opportunities for children to demonstrate their abilities and thereby minimizes the chance of failing to identify a child who may benefit from the program (Shwedel & Stoneburner, 1983). Second, the selection of formal sources of data should be based on the degree of validity that has been established for these sources. Either they should be highly correlated with established tests that measure the same trait (concurrent validity), or they should be good predictors of the child's future behavior (predictive validity). Formal sources of data that only report face or content validity should be suspect and avoided. Technical manuals of tests should include a discussion of the tests' validity. Third, formal sources of data chosen should be used with the population for which they were intended as well as in the manner in which they were intended to be used. Fourth, informal methods should have good face validity. That is, the information obtained from the informal source should be relevant to the trait or traits being measured.

Reliability

Reliability is the extent to which variations in data reflect actual variations in the phenomena under study rather than being a result of measurement error. In other words, can we be assured that the test or procedure being used will consistently produce the same results given the same input?

As with validity, there are steps that can be taken to ensure the development of a reliable identification and assessment plan. First, selection of formal sources of data should be based on the degree of reliability established for each source. Reliability coefficients should be found in the test's technical manual. Secondly, steps should be taken whenever possible to establish the reliability of informal sources of data. Both parents can be asked to fill out checklists, or it may be possible to have a teacher and aide complete the teacher checklist independently. By examining the same informal source of data completed by two individuals regarding the same child, one will be able to determine if the information obtained from this source is consistent across individuals.

Harmony

Harmony depends on whether the tests and procedures chosen are appropriate for matching the child with the program. It is possible that specific tests or procedures within an identification plan are reliable and valid but are not compatible with the goals of the program. Tests of creativity which focus on creative thinking and verbal expression would obviously not be in harmony with a program whose goals were to enhance talents in the visual and performing arts.

Practicality

One issue often overlooked is the practicality of the identification procedure. A careful balance must be maintained between the quality of the information to be obtained by the identification plan and the cost of obtaining that information. Cost in time and money should not exceed the needs of the program or the resources available.

STATE GUIDELINES INFLUENCING IDENTIFICATION METHODS

Guidelines recommended by states for defining and identifying gifted children have a profound influence on identification, assessment, and programming within those states. To examine such guidelines, the authors sent letters to directors of gifted programs in each of the states, Washington, D.C., Guam, and the Trust Territories of the Pacific requesting guidelines for operation of gifted programs in their state or territory. All territories and states except Kentucky sent their guidelines. Four states/territories (Vermont, Wisconsin, Trust Territories of the Pacific, and Wyoming) reported no gifted programs. Three others (Utah, New Hampshire, and Alabama) could not report accurate information, since guidelines were in the process of being developed. Our findings have been summarized in Appendices 3 and 4.

Examination of the policies of the remaining states revealed tremendous diversity. Although the federal definition of giftedness no longer includes psychomotor ability, twelve states will include it in their definition. In addition, another twelve states use three or fewer of the talent areas included in the federal definition. The most uniform component, indeed the only one used in every state, is a measure of intellectual ability. This stress on intellectual assessment also is consistent with identification methods used. Twenty-two states either require or strongly suggest an IQ test and/or an academic achievement test score as shown in Appendix 4. The most common scores required for identification as gifted are 2 standard deviations above the mean or an IQ score of 130. The lowest cut-off score specified is 120 (Mississippi).

Sixteen states allow the Local Education Agency (LEA) to set the standards for cognitive ability, but they require that a multi-instrument approach be used. Texas guidelines seem to summarize this philosophy:

> No single criterion, such as an IQ score, teacher nomination, or grades, can be the determining factor for selection of students to participate in the program or services. Although grades often indicate high achievement, some students who excel in various areas receive poor grades throughout their school lives. It is imperative, therefore, to recognize that grades received by some students are not always indicative of their true abilities or potential. Similarly, no single method of instruction should be used to remove a student once identified as gifted from the program to which he has been assigned.

Six states define a gifted child as above average or superior in intelligence, but they do not set standards, leaving the LEA to do so. Four states use a point system or matrix. Florida's system, for instance, specifies that a student be rated in four areas: achieve ment test data, intelligence test data, student grades, and teacher recommendations. Children are assigned between 4 and 8 points in the area of achievement and between 1 and 5 points in others. Thus, a student may receive a total maximum of 23 points. In order to be classified as gifted, a child must receive a total of 19 points. The advantages of this system are that it attempts to provide uniform and standard procedures and that a student's weakness in one area can be compensated for by strength in another. Disadvantages include its rigidity, lack of flexibility, complexity, and a tendency to discriminate against individuals with specific, narrow forms of giftedness and poor test-takers or underachievers.

Twenty-nine states have worded their guidelines to reflect some flexibility in an attempt to include minorities and handicapped students in their gifted programs: Arkansas, Arizona, California, Colorado, Connecticut, Delaware, Florida, Georgia, Kansas, Louisiana, Maine, Maryland, Massachusetts, Michigan, Missouri, Montana, Nebraska, Nevada, New Jersey, Oklahoma, Oregon, Pennsylvania, Rhode Island, South Carolina, South Dakota, Tennessee, Virginia, West Virginia, Washington, and the District of Columbia. For example, Arizona's guidelines state:

> The Governing Board may modify school curricula and adapt teaching methods, materials and techniques to provide educationally for those pupils who are gifted and possess superior intellect or advanced learning ability, or both, but may have an educational disadvantage resulting from a difficulty in writing, speaking or understanding the English language due to an environmental background wherein a language other than English is primarily or exclusively spoken.

Arizona obviously has attempted to provide for its Spanish-speaking minority as Mississippi has attempted to do for its disadvantaged population. Mississippi designates four types of gifted programs: (a) intellectually gifted, (b) disadvantaged gifted, (c) talented, and (d) gifted/handicapped. Furthermore, disadvantaged children are to be administered either the Abbreviated Binet for Disadvantaged Gifted, the Raven's Progressive Matrices, or the Leiter International Performance Scale. Of course, this sensitivity to an inclusion of minorities and handicapped children may or may not be effectively translated into LEA policy, but it does seem encouraging that the policies of many states include an awareness of the problem.

It appears that most states either have vague criteria for identifying creativity, leadership ability, psychomotor skills, and visual and performing talent or have not established any criteria at all. Twenty-five states, for instance, include leadership ability as a component of giftedness; however, no state specifies procedures for identifying leadership talent. It is extremely difficult even to write a definition of leadership ability. Iowa's definition, for example, states that "leadership ability refers to those students who possess outstanding potential or demonstrated ability to exercise influence or decision making." Commendable as such an attempt at definition may be, the result seems circular and is lacking in specific direction or guidance.

In conclusion, there seem to be two major difficulties in present identification policies. First, giftedness tends to be interpreted in various ways with varying degrees of specificity, and there seems to be little or no consensus on what elements or aspects that gifted educational programs should address. Intellectual ability and academic achievement are the most frequently addressed components. States that do include psychomotor skills, leadership, creativity, and the visual and performing arts generally do not provide a definition or criteria that gives clear guidance to identification procedures. Secondly, there seems to be difficulty establishing the balance between subjective methods and objective criteria, between overly flexible methods and techniques that are too rigid. Requiring objective tests and/or specific cut-off scores ensures a degree of uniformity throughout the system but leads to other problems. Objective methods often have proven to be inaccurate in identifying gifted students, and requirements and criteria that are too limited or specific are ineffective. Arbitrary cut-off scores and standardized tests simply are not sensitive to local needs, availability of resources, or cultural differences. On the other hand, the use of subjective instruments may lead to the inclusion of only polite, well-behaved, studious children, thus excluding many or most gifted children and creating a gifted program primarily composed of nongifted children.

On a more positive note, it seems that many state policies are sensitive to the issues involved. Many require or strongly encourage a multi-method approach to identification. The sensitivity of some states to the need for including minority, culturally diverse, and handicapped students is a positive trend. In general, guidelines seemed to be designed to provide LEA's with direction in identification procedures while allowing them the flexibility to address the particular needs and abilities of the local population.

IMPLEMENTATION OF IDENTIFICATION AND ASSESSMENT PROCEDURES AT THE UNIVERSITY OF ILLINOIS

Illustrative of effective procedures in identification and assessment of young gifted/talented handicapped and nonhandicapped children are two programs in progress at the University of Illinois. One program was initiated in 1975 with funds from the Bureau of Education for the Handicapped (BEH), now referred to as the Office of Special Education Programs (OSEP), to develop a model for the gifted/talented handicapped and is referred to as Retrieval and Acceleration of Promising Young Handicapped and Talented (RAPYHT) (Karnes, 1984a; Karnes, 1984b; Karnes & Bertschi, 1978; Karnes, Shwedel, & Linnemeyer, 1982; Karnes, Shwedel, & Lewis, 1983a; Karnes, Shwedel, & Lewis, 1983b). This project is in the outreach stage and is being replicated currently at 77 sites in 18 states. The other program, funded in 1980 by the Federal Office of the Gifted for young nonhandicapped children, was given the name of University Primary School (Uni Pri) (Karnes et al., 1985; Karnes et al., 1982; Karnes, Shwedel, & Williams, 1983). The charge of this grant was to develop and demonstrate a model program for identifying and programming for young gifted children. Both programs now are funded locally, the first by school districts in rural Champaign County and the other primarily by fees from parents. RAPYHT serves 3- to 5-year-old gifted/talented youngsters with specific disabilities, and Uni Pri serves 3- to 8-year-old nonhandicapped gifted/talented children.

RAPYHT

RAPYHT is designed to serve mildly and moderately handicapped children who have problems that interfere with learning in one of four areas—sensory, physical, social and emotional, or behaviors associated with learning deficits—and who have been identified as potentially or functionally gifted in one or more of the six areas of giftedness: intellectual, academic (science, reading, and mathematics), leadership, creativity, visual and performing arts (music and art), or psychomotor. The RAPYHT model is implemented in ongoing programs where handicapped children have been identified and where individual educational plans in the areas of handicap have been determined by an interdisciplinary team.

The RAPYHT program model consists of six components: general programming, talent screening and identification, in-depth talent assessment, linking talent assessment with talent programming, parent involvement, and evaluation.

General Programming

Currently teachers replicating the model are trained to foster creativity, higher-level thinking, problem solving, and talent in the visual and performing arts with all children in the program the first half of the year. They have access to activities which are designed to foster skills and talents associated with giftedness. Concurrently with this training, teachers also are provided training in recognizing characteristics of gifted/talented children as well as strategies for working with children to facilitate the emergence of talent. In an earlier version of RAPYHT, teachers were expected to start identifying potential candidates for the program immediately in contrast to the present practice of delaying identification until sufficient opportunity for stimulation and observation has occurred.

The new approach to identification seems to be especially valid because it gives teachers an opportunity to learn and practice new skills that foster the emergence of talent among their charges. The University of Illinois project staff recognizes that handicapping conditions tend to obscure gifts and talents and that, unless a deliberate effort is made to foster the development of skills associated with giftedness, these skills may never be manifested.

Screening and Identification

Identification of gifts and talents is considered an ongoing process. It may take weeks, months, or even years for gifts and talents to emerge to the extent that they become functional and easily observable. Then, too, the University of Illinois staff members endorse Maker (1977), who advocates that in identifying the gifted and talented, the handicapped be compared with other handicapped children first rather than with their nonhandicapped peers.

One of the first tasks undertaken by the project staff was to develop screening instruments in the six areas of giftedness and talent. Since a search of the literature did not reveal any screening instruments developed for young children who were nonhandicapped nor handicapped, task forces were set up among staff working with young handicapped children to develop such instruments. Lists of characteristics of giftedness/talents developed for older children were used, as well as opinions of experts in the field. In addition, teachers of the handicapped were consulted to determine characteristics they had noted that indicated above-average potential. Professors and doctoral students in the various areas addressed by the RAPYHT project were solicited to review and criticize the instruments and guidelines. The reliability and validity of the checklists were established. Cut-off scores for each area identified approximately 9.2% of the children as potentially or functionally gifted.

An instrument for parents was developed similar to that used by teachers. Consistently over the years parents have tended to rate their children higher than teachers did. Parents' ratings may suggest as high as 15% of the handicapped may be potentially or functionally gifted.

The RAPYHT project uses a wide net in identifying the potentially gifted. It is the feeling of the staff that it is better to err on the side of including more children as potentially eligible for the program than to overlook possible candidates. The final identification of candidates for RAPYHT intensive programming is determined by a multi-disciplinary team who consider the results of parent and teacher checklists, standardized test results, observations of children, and a list of characteristics common to gifted children. In a class of 10-15 children, only one or two may be considered for RAPYHT programming.

In-Depth Assessment

An instrument called Talent Assessment for Program Planning (TAPP) (Karnes, Steinberg, Brown, & Shwedel, 1982) has been developed to examine a child's level of functioning within each talent area, to provide information for program planning and implementation, and to evaluate the child's progress in his or her talent area. For example, in assessing artistic talent, the area is divided into visual sensitivity, technical skill, aesthetic expression, appreciation and originality.

Talent Programming

At the meeting of the interdisciplinary team where specific goals are set for each child, the teacher is able to match the child's stage of development in a talent area with specific programming using TAPP information. The teacher can then develop the objectives to accomplish the goal in the child's talent area. Activities have been developed for the teacher to use or adapt to help the child achieve the goals set for him. These activities are included in *The Talent Activities Manual* developed by Karnes and Associates (1982).

Talent programming is based on the TAPP assessment and the utilization of activities (Karnes et al., 1982) to accomplish the objectives set by the teacher and the goals delineated at the multidisciplinary staffing of the child. Following the special education plan of writing an Individual Education Plan (IEP) in the area of weakness, a Talent Education Plan (TEP) is written in the area of giftedness/talent. The *Nurturing Talent Manuals* (Karnes & Associates, 1978) in each area of talent give the teacher suggestions for helping the child enhance his or her progress in the talent area. The family is involved not only in the identification of gifts/talents but also in programming for the child. Parents are trained to foster the development of their child's talent, and written suggestions are provided for them to use with their child.

During 1984-85 the Administration of Children, Youth, and Families funded the University of Illinois to adapt the RAPYHT approach to use with Head Start children. This project has been well accepted by personnel in Head Start. Essentially, the program has been simplified so that it can be readily implemented in Head Start. We refer to this adaptation as Bringing Out Head Start Talent (BOHST). Although Head Start has been successful in identifying and programming for the average Head Start child, and in more recent years has been successful in programming for the handicapped, they have made little or no attempt to identify and program for children who are potentially gifted/talented. Thus, BOHST is the first project funded by ACYF to identify and better serve this segment of the Head Start population.

The effects of RAPYHT and BOHST programming are promising. Research data support the belief of the University of Illinois project staff that early identification and more appropriate programming do make a significant difference in the functioning of potentially or functionally gifted/talented children among the handicapped and in the Head Start population.

The University Primary School

The University Primary School serves children ages 3 through 8. The major goals for the children are the development of: (a) healthy, realistic self-concepts; (b) appropriate and effective interpersonal skills; (c) positive attitudes toward school and learning; (d) task commitment; (e) exploratory behavior and risk-taking skills; (f) creative and productive thinking; and (g) higher-level thinking processes. Goals for the parents include: (a) increased understanding of their gifted child; (b) acquiring skills as advocates for their gifted child; (c) acquiring knowledge and skills to stimulate their child's full development; (d) learning appropriate methods of child management so that their child grows up stable, happy, and productive; and (e) utilizing resources in the interests of their gifted child.

The philosophy of the University Primary School is derived from the open framework of the British Infant School and is based on five principles: (a) learning involves acting on the environment, (b) learning is developmental, (c) learning is facilitated by participation in decision making, (d) learning integrates knowledge, and (e) learning is based on dialogue.

In addition to the more informal, "open education" conceptual model, the program also uses a complementary instructional model derived from Guilford's Structure of the Intellect (Guilford, 1967). It is important to the successful implementation of the model that teachers be committed to the approach, and that parents feel it meets the needs of their gifted child.

The identification of children for the program relies almost exclusively on parent referral. To recruit candidates, an extensive advertising campaign is conducted each spring by means of fliers placed on bulletin boards in churches, university buildings, doctors' offices, libraries, and other public buildings. Announcements also are made on radio and local television. Parents are urged to contact the director of the school if they are interested. Those who call are invited to an interpretation of the program, beginning with a slide-tape presentation. Following this overview, a staff member accompanies them on a visit to a classroom. Parents are encouraged to ask questions, and before leaving they receive a packet of written materials. In addition to interpreting the goals of the school, staff members also explain how the curriculum differs from a regular curriculum. Often a parent makes a second visit, accompanied by the child, who is encouraged to participate in the activities of a classroom. Any parent who feels the program will meet the child's needs is asked to make an appointment for the child to take a battery of tests. The parent is sent a questionnaire developed by Karnes and Associates that is designed to elicit information on the child's functioning in the various talent areas, to be returned at or before the appointment.

For the 3-, 4-, and 5-year-olds, the battery of tests assess the child in the areas of intellectual, creative, and fine motor/perceptual functioning. The 6-, 7-, and 8-year-old children are given an achievement test, or achievement test data are obtained from the school where the child has been enrolled.

The three criteria for entry into the program are:

1. Scoring 1.5 standard deviations or more above the mean on any one of the standardized tests: *Goodenough-Harris Draw-A-Person Test* (Harris, 1963), *Stanford-Binet Intelligence Test* (Terman & Merrill, 1973), or *Thinking Creatively in Action and Movement* (Torrance, 1981).
2. Scoring 1.25 standard deviations or more above the mean on any two of these instruments.
3. Scoring at least 1 standard deviation above the mean on any two of these instruments, if the child is from a low socio-economic background.

The first year of the project (1980), there was one class of 3- and 4-year-olds. The second year the program was expanded to two classes. Seventy-six children were assessed during these two years, and 31 (41%) met eligibility requirements. Since that time, more effort has been made to train parents in what to look for in their children to ensure that referrals are more accurate. During the summer of 1985, 46 children were assessed to fill vacancies in three classes, and only 2 out of the 46 did not meet the criteria. With 96% meeting criteria, it seems well worth the effort to spend time training parents to be better observers of their children.

CONCLUSION

Although it may be more difficult to identify and assess very young gifted/talented children, whether handicapped or not, than older children, research and experience have enabled us to identify and to initiate programming more confidently than ever before. Researchers are sharing information by publishing their findings, demonstrating models appropriate to young gifted children, providing technical assistance to professionals at sites who wish to replicate these models, and sharing products with replication sites.

Our need now, in order to guard against loss of talent in a world which needs all the talent that can be made available, is for advocates who will influence legislators to provide financial resources for screening, identifying, and programming for young potentially or functionally gifted/talented children down to age 3. Identifying and nurturing gifts and talents to enable young children to actualize their potential is a way of improving the mental health and quality of life of such individuals. We know that a wide discrepancy between potential and full utilization of potential is a breeding ground for maladjustment and unproductivity. The need for early identification and early programming is thus manifest. Professionals in gifted education and the parents of gifted children must see that the need is met.

Recognizing Superior Cognitive Abilities in Disadvantaged, Minority, and Other Diverse Populations

Virginia Z. Ehrlich, EdD

ABSTRACT. A knowledge of the characteristics of diverse populations that may hinder identification will help to eliminate some of the obstacles to identifying the gifted among those who are not members of the dominant culture of a community. Equally important in the selection process are the recruitment procedures, criteria for selection of students, the quality of the measures used for identification, and the training and skills of the examiner/interviewers. Examples of successful identification practices utilized in the Astor Program illustrate the various approaches to identification that produced a gifted student group reflective of the demographic character of the city.

The early identification of cognitively gifted children can lead to conflict and error when some basic principles of program planning are violated. Some of these principles include (Ehrlich, 1978):

—Preparing a statement of basic philosophy in advance.
—Defining the goals of the program.
—Specifying the definition of giftedness as it applies to the program.
—Establishing criteria for recruiting and selecting students, in advance and in writing.
—Learning about the character of the population being served; recognizing cultural, ethnic, economic, and social differences.

Virginia Z. Ehrlich is Honorary Adjunct Associate Professor at Teachers College, Columbia University; Creator and Director of the Astor Program for Gifted Children, funded by the Vincent Astor Foundation; Former Director of Gifted Child Studies in New York City Public Schools; Educational Consultant and Lecturer; Author of *Gifted Children: A Guide for Parents and Teachers*, and other publications on the gifted.

A most important first step in any identification process, whether it be for the gifted or any other population, is to establish the program philosophy and goals, which depend upon the attitudes, knowledge, goals, and understandings of the planners. Second in importance is the step of clarifying the definitions and terms to be used. Defining terms, therefore, becomes an essential part of designing and initiating the planning process leading to the identification of gifted children. Let us review a few of these briefly.

SOME DEFINITIONS

Cognitive Giftedness

Cognition is defined as "the act or process of knowing, including both awareness and judgment" (Webster's, 1972). When we speak of cognitive giftedness, we are referring to exceptional capacity for acquiring and processing knowledge, especially as related to schooling and education in general. Or, it may be described as the ability that makes possible successful existence in the society in which one lives.

Most identification procedures are planned and developed from the perspective of the dominant cultural patterns of the society, supported by traits of development common to all people. A recognition of the great diversity of subpopulations that one finds in most communities requires an understanding of special groups (i.e., the disadvantaged, specific ethnic affiliations, cultural minorities, the handicapped).

The Disdavantaged

Disadvantaged applies to "an unfavorable, inferior, or prejudicial condition" (Webster's, 1972). It is a broad term that can be applied equally, for example, to children of wealthy but indifferent parents, the poor or economically deprived, the geographically isolated, the culturally different.

Ethnic Minorities

Ethnic minorities may or may not be included among the disadvantaged. It is a term that refers to "races or large groups of people classed according to common traits and customs" (Webster's,

1972), and refers to members of diverse groups within the dominant culture of the local community as well as with respect to national demographics. For example, Blacks are a numerical minority in the United States, even though they are in the numerical majority in a large local area such as Harlem in New York City.

The Handicapped

The handicapped are those who have some physical or psychological impairment that interferes with normal activities, and, therefore, may be included among the disadvantaged populations.

PROBLEMS IN RECOGNIZING COGNITIVE ABILITIES

Many of the observations made in this chapter on recognizing cognitive giftedness are based primarily on experiences with the New York City public school system and the Astor Program for gifted children, ages 4 through 8 (Ehrlich, 1978). New York City offers a great variety of experiences and settings that become applicable to other localities, including urban, suburban, and quasi-rural areas. In such a large public school system, with its varied geography, demographics, and a school population of almost one million pupils serviced by 32 school districts, it is reasonable to expect to identify large numbers of cognitively gifted children representing most of the many diverse populations residing there. For example, in one school building there are over 47 different ethnic groups represented. In planning a program for the gifted, therefore, it becomes the responsibility of administrators to try to reach as wide a sample as possible in the interest of fairness and equality of opportunity for all children.

This attitude and belief system is no less important in other, smaller communities where the demographics may be restricted in terms of numbers and variety. There are comparable percentages of individuals with cognitive giftedness to be found in all special populations except the mentally retarded. It is our responsibility to seek reliable and efficient ways of discovering those individuals. An awareness of some of the problems presented by special populations in the identification process should aid in maximizing the efficiency of our procedures. Major obstacles to recognizing cognitive abilities are related to recruitment procedures, examiner/interviewer orientation, and selection criteria.

Recruitment Procedures

Some plans for recruiting children for a special program are so designed that they automatically exclude groups. Reliance on word-of-mouth advertising is obviously inadequate and almost inevitably results in an unrepresentative selection. Alternatively, using the media that actually reach the largest number of people can help to insure a fair sampling.

The Astor Program in New York City, which pioneered the introduction of early childhood education of the gifted in a public school system, had to consider the great diversity of the city's pupil population in recruiting children. In order to publicize the program as widely as possible, we took advantage of the cooperative spirit of local foreign language radio stations and of newspapers, such as the *Chinatown News*, the *Amsterdam News* (Harlem), *El Diario* (for Hispanics), and others. Leaders within special groups and community centers also were canvassed for assistance. Additionally, a flyer was sent home via every pupil in each affected school. Although this procedure increased the number of applicants to be screened, it served to facilitate the achievement of two important program goals: (a) to provide equal opportunity for all students to qualify for participation; and (b) to reflect the diversity of the city's population in the program enrollment (Ehrlich, 1978).

Examiner/Interviewer Orientation

Still another potential obstacle to the identification of cognitively gifted children in special populations can be the orientation or experiential background of the interviewer, psychologist, or test examiner. Too often school psychologists and guidance counselors spend so much time focusing on reported learning problems and misbehavior that their observations of the exceptionally gifted child become negatively biased. They see the problems, the "failings" of the child, and lose sight of the forces operating in the youngster's life that arise from the very fact that he or she may be gifted.

In the Astor Program, I found that I had to reorient school psychologists and others who gave me reports that would have normally excluded such children from the very program that was designed to avoid or overcome the causes of the children's misbehavior. For example, we were advised not to take Tommy, age 4, because he had been "expelled" from nursery school, was rambunctious and uncooperative, and in general seemed emotionally disturbed. He was being given Ritalin as a sedative. His measured IQ was over 150. An interview with his mother elicited from her comments to this effect: "We can't control him. He gets into everything, breaks all his toys because he wants to know how they are made. He's a nuisance, forever asking questions. Even when his father takes a strap to him, he won't stop!" Needless to say, we included Tommy in our program. With the help of a generously patient teacher and a class encouraged to be kind and caring, Tommy soon learned that asking questions and being curious was "OK," that he was "an OK boy" for being so eager to learn, and therefore it was unnecessary to rebel or cry out for attention in a less cooperative manner.

Selection Criteria: Subjective Measures

Still another potential obstacle to identifying the cognitively gifted children from special subpopulations during the early years lies in the criteria used for selection with either subjective or objective measures. Many procedures that may be suitable for older children, particularly from the majority culture and advantaged population, are basically inappropriate for the very young child. Included among those subjective measures of identification are both teacher and peer nomination.

Teacher Nomination

The prekindergarten/kindergarten teacher usually has little basis for an informed judgment about a child's specific cognitive abilities simply because the opportunities for observing them are so limited during the first months of schooling, and because there are usually very limited, if any, records of the child's specific intellectual performance in prior school experiences. In fact, research has shown that teachers tend to be very poor identifiers of giftedness at this stage (Ciha, 1974; Jacobs, 1971), which may be attributed to a lack of needed information about the child's potentialities.

Another aspect of teacher nomination that may make it inefficient as an identification tool is the fact that too many teachers at all levels rarely recognize even the highly gifted child if other behaviors are less than desirable or below the norm. It is only when teachers are given intensive training and guidance in how to identify gifted students that their efficiency is improved. A frequent cause of their difficulty in recognizing giftedness may be a failure to create classroom conditions that elicit and reward higher intellectual behavior. Nevertheless, in a study conducted by this author with parents, teachers, and Astor Program pupils, I found that, even after years of training, few teachers recognized their brightest students; they tended to rank them somewhere in the middle of the class (Ehrlich, 1981).

Peer nomination

A second identification procedure that is not effective at this stage is peer nomination. Just as in the case of teacher nomination, the opportunities for observing and understanding the intellectual behavior of other children may be based on too brief a period of acquaintanceship and limited forms of interaction. Furthermore, young children are not ready to make such critical comparisons in any reliable, objective way.

Selection Criteria: Objective Measures

Objective measures used for identification of the cognitively gifted include a wide variety of test instruments, administered either individually or in groups. The services of specialists trained in the area are required for appropriate selection and administration of such tests. The major problems posed by the use of objective measures, however, include the possibility of test bias, the inappropriate use of test results, and ignoring important criteria for test selection.

Test Bias

There is much concern that objective measures or tests that are used may be biased against special populations. Unfortunately, often it is not the test that is biased but rather that the examiner has not done his/her homework. It is the responsibility of planners to see that the selection of a test is appropriate for the age level and the population concerned. Information about the characteristics, purposes, effectiveness, and limitations of published tests is available from the publishers. The best known and most reliable references on published tests are the Buros Mental Measurement Yearbooks (Buros, 1972). Discussions of tests also appear in texts by Anastasi (1976) and by Thorndike and Hagen (1977). A review of tests designed for this age level appeared in *Educating the Pre-School/Primary Gifted and Talented* (Ehrlich, 1980). A frequently expressed specific objection to IQ tests is that they are culturally biased. There is, in fact, no "culture free" test. In identifying superior cognitive abilities, one is restricted to those behaviors that make for successful existence within the dominant culture in which one lives and/or behaviors that are characteristic of the universe of human beings. Thus, individual IQ tests, such as the Stanford-Binet or the WICS-R, rely on physical developmental patterns to some extent for evaluating superior ability during the early years. Other items sample general behaviors related to cognition presented in a setting familiar to most children, regardless of cultural origins. The tests are reviewed and updated at frequent intervals. The Stanford-Binet has just been updated to overcome biases that may have been present in the norming sample used in earlier editions (Thorndike, 1985).

Inappropriate Use of Test Scores

Another source of problems arising from the use of objective tests lies in their administration with total reliance on an impersonal objectivity, where practical judgment seems suspended. In other words, if the results of testing contradict the informed observations of the examiner, there should be a questioning or an inquiry into the source of the discrepancy with an openness to the possibility that observed behaviors are more reliable indicators of giftedness than are the test scores. While testing young children for eligibility for the Astor Program, our judgment occasionally disagreed with the "objective" result. In one case, for example, little Mei-ling, a Chinese child who was not quite 4-years-old had impressed all of us with her advanced cognitive ability. I remember, especially, her asking me whether those whitish plants on my windowsill could possibly be coleus, since they did not have the pretty pinkish colors she associated with the plant. Yes, indeed, I explained, they were coleus, but a special kind.

When Mei-ling was tested, the results were good (IQ about 125), but much lower than we had expected. Normally, she would not be included in our program because of limited space. Feeling strongly about our own observations, we pursued the matter and learned from her mother, who spoke perfect English, that Mei-ling rarely spoke English since she lived with her grandparents who spoke Chinese only. Relying on judgment based on our years of experience with such children, we accepted this child into the program. Within a few months, a re-test confirmed our judgment that this "bilingual" child had a "corrected" IQ score of 157. Obviously, the arbitrary acceptance of objective data, without the application of informed judgment, can lead to errors in identification.

Criteria for Selecting Appropriate
Test Instruments (Ehrlich, 1980)

These criteria should guide planners in the selection of tests used to identify cognitive giftedness in young children:

1. Objectivity
2. Statistical reliability
3. Statistical and construct validity
4. Historical record of success in identification and predictability
5. Appropriateness of language
6. Cultural appropriateness
7. Cost of administration
8. Time required to administer
9. Quality of standardization sample
10. Pupil behaviors sampled by the test

CULTURAL PATTERNS INFLUENCING SELECTION PROCEDURES

There are still other factors that must be considered in the identification process. These are related to special characteristics of diverse populations that can affect the efficiency of the procedures used. It is obviously impossible to list all such influences, but citing a few may serve to create awareness. Following are a few examples of cultural patterns that influence either testing results or the general recruitment and identification process. Although the examples are derived primarily from experiences with the Astor Program and other gifted programs in New York City, some have been gleaned from extensive correspondence and experience with other communities in the United States and abroad.

Oriental Children

In recruiting children for the Astor Program from our extensive Chinese community, we found that children were not responding readily to the examiner. Upon inquiry, we learned that the Chinese and other Oriental families stress modesty, especially in girls. The children hesitated to answer questions "knowledgeably" lest they seem to be unduly boastful. We were fortunate in having the services of an understanding Cantonese lady, whose presence during the interviews and testing reassured the children.

American Indian Children

American Indian children are trained to exhibit cooperative behavior. Educators in areas close to reservations or including large American Indian populations have found that the children will help each other during group testing when they are in difficulty, a behavior which is generally viewed as "cheating" by the dominant culture.

Bilingualism

Bilingualism in the home is common among immigrant groups. Their children learn to use two languages, with varying levels of proficiency in each. Proficiency in English tends to lag when other than familial situations are encountered. In recruiting among such groups, it is important to consider these factors in evaluating the children's abilities. For example, when a mother brought us her 4-year-old son because she was convinced that he was gifted, we were amazed that she, in fact, spoke practically no English. Her son interpreted for her into accented but good English. We asked him how he had learned to speak the language and to read so well at this tender age. We found that he was completely self-taught, having learned from television and the newspapers. He, like Mei-ling, did only moderately well on our objective test (IQ about 120); but, on retesting after a few months in our program, he attained a score over 140.

Pacing

Still another cultural pattern which affects pupil responses is pacing. Many groups do not respond well to timed evaluative procedures. We found this to be true among inner city Black children as well as those from families originating in southerly climates. Proper preparation for the requirements of a testing situation is required when dealing with these children, especially in group test situations.

Family Ties

We found that many families, especially Puerto Ricans, do not like to have their children travel great distances from home, particularly during the early years. They prefer to have their children as near to home as possible. This reason alone prevented many parents from including their children in a program that involved some traveling.

Sex Roles

There are many groups that view the sexes differently in terms of school advancement and achievement. Many do not recognize giftedness in their little girls and do not seem to be as concerned about providing them with the same opportunities they seek for their boys.

SPECIAL SITUATIONS

There are also special situations, unrelated to cultural backgrounds, that affect the recruitment and identification process.

Parents With Limited Education

The behavior of parents with limited education may not be consistent with the high aspirations they have for their children. Lack of experience with the educational process makes it difficult for them to align their priorities and conform to the demands of special programs that may not follow the established and known school practices.

Parents of Superior Ability/Education

Strangely, yet understandably, parents with superior ability and/or higher education tend to expect too much of their children, to assume their gifted behavior is "normal," and to underestimate their specific higher abilities. This also happens in families where the first born is gifted, and the behavior of younger siblings is measured against the higher standards of the oldest child and interpreted as being normal rather than gifted. In families of gifted children, it frequently occurs that the first-born tends to receive the most attention while younger siblings' abilities tend to be overlooked.

Pressured Children

Disadvantaged (as defined earlier) gifted children can be found in all economic levels, ethnic and social groups. Parent personalities, lifestyles, and cultural patterns affect their expectations for their children. Among these we find the "pressured" child, who is pushed to achieve because of parental pride and competitiveness. In testing situations, such children frequently respond to the understanding approach of the examiner by withdrawing and pretending not to know answers or by not even trying to respond. One little girl we encountered responded consistently with "I don't know" to most questions, when it was apparent that she knew the answers and could perform at much higher levels. An awareness of this phenomenon by the examiner is important if such children are not to be overlooked during the recruitment process.

Indifferent Parents

Probably one of the most difficult situations to comprehend is the case of economically advantaged parents who are well educated but who seem to be indifferent to the emotional, social, and developmental needs of their children. These neglected but economically affluent children are disadvantaged by a lack of needed intellectual stimulation and frequently are overlooked as potentially gifted simply because their intellectual deprivation is so inconsistent with the expectations held for parents of such social status.

Handicapped Children

It is likely that the largest number of overlooked gifted children will be found among the handicapped. There is a tendency on the part of both parents and professionals to focus on the negative aspects of being handicapped rather than on the positive qualities of potential giftedness. Broad generalizations about particular handicaps also hinder the identification process. For example, spina bifida is frequently accompanied by a certain amount of retardation. A family I admired greatly for their management of their child's handicap was nevertheless surprised to learn that their little girl had an IQ of 175+. Fortunately, while giving full attention to her physical needs, they were equally careful to nurture the child's remarkable intellectual abilities.

Developmental and Maturational Factors

One also should note the importance of a thorough awareness of developmental and maturational factors that influence early childhood behavior (Terrassier, 1979). Too many children are labelled "language disabled" during the early years, for example, when in fact time and maturation is all that is needed to overcome the so-called disability. Professionals in the special education field are greatly concerned by the excessive numbers of such children so labeled (Shepard, 1984). For example, early difficulties in learning to read and write or to follow directions dependably often obscure from the perceptions of adults indicators of giftedness in young children.

Premature Schooling

There also are parents who insist on involving their children in formal schooling situations long before they are socially or emotionally ready. The immature behavior and lack of adjustment of the child may interfere with recognition of his/her giftedness. Although many gifted children do enjoy the stimulating environment of a well planned preschool program, there are many others who need the one-to-one relationship with their mothers and a few more years enjoying the security of the home base. Parents need reassurance that delaying formal schooling in such situations will do no harm and, in fact, may be the more desirable alternative. Such a decision by parents, however, will affect recruitment efforts.

Fear of Being Different

In years of responding as director of gifted programs for the New York City Board of Education to parents' inquiries concerning their gifted children, I found that one of the most frequent concerns expressed by them was a desire to protect their children from a situation that might accentuate their "differentness." Basically, parents wanted to protect their children from conditions where their brightness might alienate them from the rest of the peer group. At all costs, they wanted to avoid putting their children under any excessive pressure simply because they were gifted. Often, all they really wanted was reassurance that any decision they might make concerning their children's involvement or noninvolvement in a gifted program would not endanger the development of their children's abilities.

MISLEADING CHILD BEHAVIORS

There also are some misleading behaviors that can interfere with accurate identification of young children as gifted. These include the very verbal child, the conformist, the exceptionally well-behaved child, the pushed child who shows advanced achievement in reading and some arithmetic. Without objective confirmation, children demonstrating such behavior may be considered gifted when, in reality, they may be reflecting family pressure. Such children may reach a peak of performance which levels off early in the schooling process.

There also are some negative behaviors that may lead one to overlook a potentially gifted child. These are traits that frequently influence both parents and teachers to consider the child "nongifted." Clues that one should look for include: withdrawal or excessive shyness; inattentiveness; poor achievement; lack of interest in reading; truancy, high absenteeism and tardiness; defiance; cultural reserve (certain ethnic groups); clowning, demanding attention; and leadership of a negative type, such as making trouble.

RELIABLE INDICATORS
OF COGNITIVE GIFTEDNESS

Having been forewarned of all the pitfalls inherent in the identification procedures, one may hesitate even to undertake such an effort. But, accurately identifying young gifted children to participate in an appropriate educational program is, in fact, possible and a gratifying experience. In the Astor Program, where we had to process hundreds of applications for an initial capacity of sixty pupils, our greatest disappointment was in having to reject so many children only because we did not have space. The children were tested on entry to the program and on subsequent occasions, and we found that our evaluation data were efficient and remarkably consistent over a three-year period. Unusual discrepancies among data were investigated, and we found that most could be explained by unusual events such as family crises or illness. The identification procedures used for this program have been described in detail elsewhere (Ehrlich, 1978). We were able to conclude that there are reliable indicators of giftedness, both objective and subjective, for this age group and the special subpopulations of New York City.

Among the objective techniques used for identification in the Astor Program, we found that the Stanford-Binet Intelligence Scale remains the most reliable and valid standardized instrument for children at this age level and across diverse populations. It seems much more efficient than less rigorously developed checklists and observational techniques. We had an opportunity to check this by including a group in the program for whom a different set of identification criteria was used (Ehrlich, 1978). We also found that the Wechsler Intelligence Scale for Children-Revised (WICS-R) is a good second choice, but seems to be less discriminating at higher levels of intellectual ability. The Goodenough Draw-A-Man Test, which takes so little time to administer, is a good confirmatory adjunct to the individual tests and also gives some projective information. A reliable reading readiness test helps to evaluate pupil achievement, especially since many exceptionally bright children are self-taught readers. Over sixty percent of children admitted to the Astor Program could read at ages four and five, although this was not a requirement for admission.

We first observed, and later confirmed by statistical analysis, that parents can be excellent identifiers of their gifted children. Although they cited as many as 35 traits in describing why they thought their children were gifted, we found that just a few (seven) were significantly correlated with superior ability as measured by the Stanford-Binet (Ehrlich, 1981). The analysis yielded these significant traits mentioned most often by parents: reading ability, insight, exceptional vocabulary, thinking ability, capacity for symbolic thought, sensitivity, and early development. And, the brighter the child, the greater the number of these significant traits that were cited.

Although the literature includes numerous studies reporting the use of checklists of various kinds, none has yielded a reliable set of traits that can be used as a unit to identify giftedness at this stage. The Astor Program research cited above was an attempt to fill this gap, but much follow-up and cross-validation will be needed before it can be used with assurance of reliability and validity. Following the principle that multiple criteria must be used in identifying the gifted, especially during the early years, the Astor Program combined use of the individual IQ test, a reading readiness test, and parent nomination with the psychologists' observations, a biographical and health questionnaire, recommendations from teachers, pediatricians and other professionals, and an interview with both parent and child.

CONCLUSIONS

An awareness of the many problems inherent in the identification process, especially for populations different from the dominant culture, should not be a deterrent in undertaking the planning and development of programs for the gifted during the early preschool/primary grade years. The outstanding success of the Astor Program in identifying children equitably representing very diverse populations and the positive results of systematic studies evaluating the efficiency and accuracy of the identification methods used are testimony to the fact that not only can cognitively gifted children be identified successfully at an early age but that techniques are available for attaining excellent representation of children from many special populations. An analysis of the Astor Program participants demonstrated that they reflected fairly accurately the demographic structure of the city (Ehrlich, 1978).

Certain conclusions can be derived from the success of the Astor Program:

1. Gifted children can be identified with reasonable accuracy during the early preschool years.
2. There are no short cuts. Identification procedures must take into account the nature of the populations being served and provide for overcoming any deterrents to obtaining a fair representation of all community populations.
3. Those responsible for the introduction of such programs must place strong reliance on the use of multiple criteria for identi-

fication, which must be administered and interpreted by well-trained and informed personnel.

4. Administrators, planners, legislators, and school boards must accept the fact that the identification process is crucial to inaugurating and maintaining successful programs for gifted children and that substantial funding must be invested in the process.

PART III:
EFFECTIVE TECHNIQUES OF NURTURING THE DEVELOPMENT OF INTELLECTUAL GIFTEDNESS

Introduction

Parents and other family members are the young child's first educators who affect the development of the child's potentialities by limiting or expanding and enriching the informal learning opportunities for him/her. The daycare or preschool teacher may be the child's first formal educator who more systematically guides the child's development through structured opportunities involving other children. Throughout the critical early years of development, parents and teachers influence the child's development in all areas through stimulation, challenge, direction, discipline, responses to the child's expressed interests and needs, and direct teaching.

The role of the educator, parent or teacher, in the early years is to help the child explore and discover the nature of his/her potential abilities, and the pleasure or satisfaction derived from developing and using those abilities. As the child becomes aware of his/her potentialities, the educator should help the child formulate a vision of rewarding outcomes if those abilities are further developed, thereby encouraging him/her to develop them. Encouragement is best provided as parents and teachers help the child structure a healthy self-concept and sense of efficacy based on a realistic assessment of personal strengths and weaknesses, develop intrinsic motivation to develop his/her giftedness, and explore career options for the future if those abilities are developed. Children as young as

71

four or five years of age enjoy exploring careers and considering how they might, as adults, utilize their special abilities. Career exploration is particularly effective in motivating the learning of gifted children in the kindergarten and primary grades.

There is no simple formula for effective parenting and teaching; it is a complex interactive process involving many factors (i.e., the child's motivational characteristics and specific needs), the personality and instructional skills of the adults, and the adequacy of the environments of home and school in relation to emotional support and intellectual stimulation. In the first article of this section, Linda Silverman will provide guidelines for effective parenting that have been derived not only from her research but from her professional interaction with young children and their families through the testing and evaluation clinic she directs in Colorado. In the second article, Margie Kitano, director of a preschool gifted program in New Mexico, will describe educational options that will assist parents and teachers in selecting or evaluating alternative programs available.

Parenting Young Gifted Children

Linda Kreger Silverman, PhD

ABSTRACT. The first step in effective parenting of gifted children is the recognition of their special abilities. The article begins by presenting a list of characteristics frequently found in young gifted children. Research is presented which shows that siblings are usually quite close in IQ, although second children may be difficult to identify since they tend to behave quite differently from firstborns. Other issues discussed include the possible depression of IQ scores in children who have suffered recurrent ear infections in the first three years of life, the importance of understanding introversion, the dangers of "normalizing" gifted children, the need for gifted peers, and the difference between "pushy" and responsive parenting. The article concludes with a list of specific guidelines for parents of young gifted children.

It has long been recognized that parents play a critical role in their children's development. For this reason, extensive parent involvement has been solicited as a standard component of the education of exceptional children in all exceptionalities save one, the gifted. Parents of gifted children are generally uninformed and excluded from the identification and education of their children. Only in recent years have parents of gifted children been allowed to know their children's IQ scores and other test results, or been asked to participate in the identification process. Historically, their input has been viewed as more intrusive than essential.

Instead of positive guidelines for successfully parenting a gifted child, most parents receive only negative admonitions from professionals and friends. Don't teach them at home or they'll be bored in school. Don't put them in school early or they'll be misfits. Don't put them in classes with other gifted children or they'll become snobs. Don't let them know they are gifted or they'll get swelled

Linda Kreger Silverman is a licensed psychologist, Director of the Gifted Child Testing Service, and Assistant Professor at the University of Denver, Denver, Colorado. She has a major textbook in preparation with Charles E. Merrill Publishing Company, *Gifted Education: A Developmental Approach.*

heads. Don't let them be alone too much or they won't develop social skills. And, don't let them pursue their interests too early or they'll be too narrow. The "Do's" are few and far between.

This article will review some basic issues related to parenting the gifted, discuss several new research areas, and present a set of parenting guidelines. The guidelines are based upon 20 years of listening to and counseling parents of gifted children, and working with 500 families who brought their children to the Gifted Child Testing Service in Denver, Colorado for assessment. In these two decades, I have developed enormous respect for parents of gifted children. They have had to rely upon their intuitive judgment of what is right for their children, without benefit of appropriate guidance and often while being bombarded by bad advice from well-meaning friends and relatives. They sometimes have faced derision by school administrators who refused to take them seriously. Often, they have been made to feel they had to accept blame for their children's perfectionism, poor risk-taking abilities, and lack of adjustment to unchallenging school situations. However, in spite of a generally unsupportive milieu, the parents with whom I have worked have done an admirable job of nurturing their children's talents. In the remainder of this article, I will share insights I have gleaned about parenting from following the lives of gifted children and listening to the wisdom of their parents.

BASIC ISSUES RELATED TO EFFECTIVE PARENTING

Recognizing Giftedness

The first step in effective parenting of a gifted child is recognition of his or her advanced abilities. Contrary to some contemporary beliefs, giftedness manifests itself quite early in life. Among the signs reported most frequently by parents of young children are the following:

- —unusual alertness
- —long attention span
- —high activity level
- —less need for sleep

—smiling or recognizing caretakers early
—advanced progression through developmental milestones
—keen sense of observation
—extreme curiosity
—excellent memory
—early and extensive vocabulary development
—intense interest in books
—rapid learning ability
—abstract reasoning
—high degrees of sensitivity
—perfectionism
—excellent sense of humor
—preference for older companions
—advanced ability in play with puzzles, mazes, or numbers

When many of these signs are present, it is likely that the child is intellectually gifted.

Children who fit these descriptors should be professionally assessed during the preschool years. Like other exceptionalities, early identification can facilitate appropriate educational placement and programming for the full development of a child's abilities. In addition, parents often need the validation of their observations that professional assessment can provide. Much of the concern about the relative unreliability of test scores for young children is based upon the difficulties of gaining cooperation during testing from the average 3- or 4-year-old; however, scores obtained on gifted preschoolers are usually more accurate (particularly high scores) than scores obtained on nongifted youngsters of the same age. Since gifted 4-year-olds have mental capabilities similar to 6-year-olds, they are mature enough to be able to follow the directions of the examiner and to concentrate on the tasks they are given. Gifted girls, in particular, should be tested early, before they begin to hide their abilities (Silverman, in press).

In the last 5 years, I have found that when parents saw signs of advanced development in their children and brought them for testing, the children almost invariably performed in the gifted range. In a study of the first 95 children brought for assessment, 95% of the children had IQs in excess of 120, 75% were beyond 132, and 25% were beyond 150. The 5% who did not test in the gifted range had some signs of giftedness and some signs of learning disability, and thus could be classified as gifted/handicapped. In another study, 21 parents sought testing after reading descriptors similar to those listed above in a local newspaper article. Over 90% of these parents had children in at least the "mildly" gifted range (above 120 IQ) (Silverman, Chitwood, & Waters, 1986b).

Dealing With the "Nongifted" Child in the Family

Many parents are reluctant to identify one of their children as gifted for fear of the effects of this diagnosis on the rest of the children in the family. One researcher (Cornell, 1983) has found some basis for this concern. Cornell studied families in which one child was designated as gifted by the schools and the siblings were not labeled as such. Not too surprisingly, he found a great deal of sibling rivalry in these families. He also found a higher incidence of friction between the parents when the mothers tending to believe the diagnosis while the fathers tended to be skeptical of the gifted label.

My own experience with the Gifted Child Testing Service sheds a somewhat different light on this phenomenon. We have found rather consistently that when one child in the family has been formally identified as intellectually gifted, all of the siblings brought for testing also qualify as gifted. Of 50 sets of siblings, we have tested, only eight contained one gifted and one nongifted child. In most cases in which a sibling did not perform in the gifted range on a standardized test, one of three variables was present: (a) one of the siblings was over 9 years old; (b) one of the siblings was 3 years old or less; or (c) one of the siblings had a history of serious ear infections early in life. The significance of these factors will be discussed later.

Moreover, we have found siblings to be remarkably close in IQ scores as derived from the same standard measures. In our sample, over one-third (19) were within five IQ points of being the same; almost two-thirds (30) were within ten IQ points; and fewer than one-third (19) were more than ten IQ points apart. When siblings are the same age at the time of the testing, are tested on the same instrument, and have had no history of chronic ear infections, their IQ scores are likely to be within 5 to 10 points of each other. It would follow that a gifted child who is viewed as "nongifted" would resent a brother or sister who is recognized and labelled as gifted.

How is it, then, that so many gifted siblings escape identification?

We have found evidence of four major sources of the problem: (a) lack of awareness that giftedness runs in families, (b) testing effects, (c) birth order effects, and (d) effects of severe early ear infections. Each of these factors is discussed briefly below.

Lack of Awareness

Since neither parents nor educators have been aware of how similar family members are apt to be in cognitive ability, they may not look for signs of giftedness in the brothers and sisters of gifted children. One leader in gifted education, however, did seem to be aware of this relationship. Dr. John Gowan traditionally allowed siblings to enroll in his creativity workshops for gifted children at San Fernando Valley State College when only one child in the family had been formally identified. As an instructor in these workshops for ten years, I could never tell which children were the "real" gifted children and which were the siblings. Now I know why I had this difficulty.

Testing Effects

Gifted children frequently have depressed IQ scores. Everyone can think of a myriad of reasons why a child might do less well on a particular test than he/she is capable of doing (e.g., not feeling well, poor rapport with the examiner, unwilling to cooperate, etc.). In addition to these factors, we have found that age at the time of testing makes a substantial difference in scores. The greatest discrepancy we found among siblings was when the two children were tested at the age of 3, and one was too immature to understand what was going on. The difference in their scores was 34 points (more than 2 standard deviations).

It is relatively easy to understand how a 3-year-old might be too young to get an accurate IQ score, but it is less clearly understood how a 9-year-old gifted child might be too old to get an accurate assessment of intelligence. We have found that the scores of most gifted children are considerably lower after the age of 9, simply because of ceiling effects (Silverman, 1986a). None of the tests currently available seems to have a high enough ceiling of difficulty to capture dependably the full range of the highly gifted child's knowledge. For example, one child we tested attained a score of 155 at 8, and 130 at 10. There were much greater discrepancies between the scores of siblings when one child was under 9 and the other was over 9 at the time of testing. The average IQ difference in eight sets of these siblings was 16 points, a full standard deviation, while the average difference for the siblings who were over 3 and under 9 was 10.

Birth Order Effects

There is a great deal of literature indicating that giftedness most often visits first children (Barbe, 1956; Cox, 1977; Goddard, 1928; Goertzel, Goertzel, & Goertzel, 1978; Hollingworth, 1926; Terman, 1925). When we began the testing service, I quite agreed with this view. Of the first 40 gifted children who came to us for testing, 70% were first-born. Then a few of the parents brought in their second children, and much to our surprise and the parents' surprise, these children's scores were almost identical to those of their older siblings. The parents were puzzled because their second children were ''so different'' from the first-borns that they didn't seem gifted at all. By the time we had tested 500 children, we saw that this situation was the norm. Most parents would have brought in only their eldest child for identification if we had not informed them of our observations that giftedness tends to run in families.

We have come to believe that there is a ''second child syndrome'' that makes giftedness very hard to recognize in those children. Whatever the first child does, the second child seems to do the opposite. If the first child is a high achiever in school, the second child doesn't seem to care much about school. If the eldest is intense, the second is easy-going. If the first-born has no friends, the second-born is everyone's buddy. If the first child is a clutz, the second child is an athlete. If the first one plays the violin, the second one appears to be tone deaf. It's as if second children go out of their way to be different from the older siblings, to establish their own identity in the world.

When teachers and parents, therefore, look for the classic signs of giftedness, they are more likely to find them in the unencumbered behavior of the first-born children in the family. These characteristics will not be as easy to recognize in the second-born child, who is desperately trying to be different from his/her older brother or sister. If it is expected, however, that siblings might be close in IQ, these second children might be coaxed out of hiding to demonstrate their capabilities.

Severe Early Ear Infection

One of the most interesting discoveries we have made in testing gifted children over the past 5 years is in the impact of early ear infections on underachievement. We have found many gifted children with hidden auditory handicaps. Most of these children suffered chronic or severe ear infections in the first three years of life. We are now in the midst of ongoing research investigating the relationship between early ear infections and underachievement. Following is a brief overview of some of our preliminary findings.

We have found that gifted children who had serious ear infections early in life have difficulty with simpler concepts and rote memorization (e.g., computation, phonics, spelling, handwriting, following directions, remembering the days of the week), but do very well with complex concepts, vocabulary, and abstract reasoning (e.g., geometry, physics, computers, poetry, creative writing). Because of their difficulties with the usual rote memorization tasks of elementary school, they suffer from poor self-concepts; they also seem to get smarter as they get older as the work gets harder. These children are often kept out of gifted programs because they do poorly with the regular schoolwork and tend to finish it very slowly. Yet, when they are placed in gifted or accelerated classes, they blossom (Baum, 1984; Whitmore, 1980). We consider these children ''gifted/handicapped,'' their gifts are hidden by their auditory disabilities, and their disabilities are masked by their giftedness. The net result is that they appear ''average'' in intellectual ability.

We have discovered some techniques that help these children to be more successful. From the onset of each ear infection until 3 months after each episode, parents should gain eye contact with the child and speak louder. Amplification prevents auditory deprivation during the critical language acquisition period. Since the visual system develops more power to compensate for the auditory deficits, parents and teachers should present information to these children visually. The children are much more likely to remember what they see rather than what they hear, and they may need more learning time. For these reasons, computers are a wonderful learning aid for gifted/handicapped children. They should learn the keyboard as soon as possible, and be allowed to use a word processor for their assignments.

Some of these children actually have a residual conductive hearing loss that has gone undetected, so it is important to have their hearing tested thoroughly by a qualified audiologist. If these children are taught (and parented) in the same way that one might teach a hearing-impaired child, the positive results obtained can be dramatic. For more information on this subject, please see "Hunting the Hidden Culprit in Underachievement: Is it Ear Infections?" (Silverman, in preparation-b).

"Normalizing" Gifted Children

One often hears that everyone wants a gifted child. In my experience, this is a myth. Most of the parents I have worked with want a "normal" child above all else. These comments are typical:

> "I don't want my child to be a freak."
> "He needs to get along with all kinds of people in this world."
> "I just want her to have friends and be happy."
> "All I want is for my child to be NORMAL."
> (Silverman, in preparation-a).

Being gifted means being different, and most parents want to protect their children from the pain of being different. Giftedness also is equated with being "abnormal," the label parents most dread. The hardest part of my job is trying to convince parents not to "normalize" their children—that is, not to try to make their children be just like everybody else. In order for human beings to develop to their fullest potential, their gifts or differences must be recognized and nurtured. I have parents imagine what would have happened if Isaac Stern's mother had just wanted him to be a normal little boy and took away his violin.

It is sometimes not understood that adjustment in childhood and adulthood are entirely different. Adults choose to associate with others of similar interests, abilities, sensitivities, and appreciations. Their friends are those who genuinely enjoy their company, who laugh with them and not at them. Finding one's true peers, however, is rarely an easy task, particularly early in life. Those who play chess and love Mahler may be very lonely in elementary school and may only find each other in an advanced mathematics class in high school. The American dream of everyone "fitting in" with everyone else simply is not the way adult lives are constructed. We fit in with those who are most like ourselves.

In childhood, however, opportunities to find others like oneself may be very limited. In order for gifted children to attempt to blend in with their classmates, they often feel they have to hide or deny their giftedness. Children cannot be gifted and "average" simultaneously. They may appear to be doing so since gifted children can, and often do, pretend to be like average children. But, at what expense? If one has the potential for outstanding achievement, the fear of being mediocre is as strong as the fear of being different. Gifted females, in particular, often choose to hide rather than to develop their exceptional abilities, so that by the time many of them reach adulthood they no longer believe they ever had unusual potential (Silverman, in preparation-a). There is even some question as to whether adults who have not developed their potential can be considered gifted or whether their giftedness is permanently lost (Borland, in press; Gallagher, 1979).

Adults who have developed their special talents usually have had parents who supported and nurtured their giftedness in childhood (Bloom, 1985). They helped them to find other children with similar abilities, and provided a rich family life to offset some of the loneliness in school (Goertzel & Goertzel, 1962). Achieving women often had lonely childhoods (Sanford, 1956) and their parents (particularly fathers) held high expectations for them (Kranz, 1975; Lemkau, 1983; Sanford, 1956).

This does not mean that all gifted children are destined for loneliness; on the contrary, they may have delightful, happy, well-adjusted childhoods, complete with many meaningful friendships, *particularly when they are helped to find gifted peers*. Gifted children will be more apt to laugh at the same jokes, share similar dreams and interests. They experience their lives as "normal" when they are with others like themselves. There is absolutely no support for the claims that placing gifted children together creates elitism or snobbery, or inability to appreciate the "common man" (Newland, 1976). These fears seem to be based upon a pervasive anti-intellectualism in our society. Talented football players are not prevented from associating with each other for fear of creating an elitist group; why, then, this irrational fear of congregations of talented artists and mathematicians?

Understanding Introversion

One way in which parents try to normalize their children is by attempting to turn introverted children into extraverts. Introversion often carries a negative connotation in people's minds, but this prejudice is unwarranted and detrimental. Since 75% of American society is extraverted (Bradway, 1964), the introvert is a member of a little-understood minority group. Understanding introversion is particularly important in teaching and parenting the gifted; in my work with gifted children, I have found that the brighter the child, the more likely he or she is to be introverted.

Introversion is a basic personality trait in which individuals gain energy from being alone rather than from being with others. Introverts feel drained by too much association with others; they need to retreat from the world to regain their sense of balance. Extraverts gain energy from being with people, the more they relate to others, the more energy they have for themselves. In a society that places a high premium on extraversion, the introvert is often at a distinct disadvantage. The "life of the party" is held up as the ideal, and the person who would rather retire with a good book is devaluaed. Although neither personality type is inherently better than the other, few mothers chide their budding socialites to spend more time alone, while happy readers are frequently admonished to be more social. Introverts receive many messages throughout their lives that their natural ways of being are inferior, and many feel the need to hide their introversion. Unfortunately, doing so has detrimental effects on their self-concepts.

Research has shown there are many differences in the ways extraverts and introverts approach situations (Jung, 1938; Keirsey & Bates, 1978; Myers, 1962). Introverts are very private individuals; they reveal their innermost feelings and thoughts to only a few intimates. Extraverts have little need for privacy, and may unthinkingly reveal the entrusted thoughts of their introverted friends, simply because they have no deep appreciation of secrecy. Because of their need for privacy, introverts develop a public persona or mask that is different from their private personality, whereas extraverts tend to be the same in public and in private. Extraverts enjoy having many friends, while introverts require only a few trusted friends throughout life. Extraverts make friends rapidly, and also may be quick to drop friendships. Introverts take a long time to develop a friendship, but once they have made a friend, it may be a lifelong relationship.

The major dread of introverts is appearing foolish, they humiliate easily. For this reason, they often are not high risk-takers, particularly in public. They are reflective, thinking through their ideas very thoroughly before sharing them with others. In contrast, extraverts tend to think on their feet, since they understand their own thoughts better as they share them orally with others. They may interrupt others or even interrupt themselves, changing the direction of their thoughts in mid-sentence, whereas introverts rarely interrupt and hate being interrupted. Extraverts learn by doing, and appear more spontaneous. Introverts learn by watching and mentally rehearsing even physical acts before they attempt them. They sometimes skip the stages of learning to walk, talk, read, or ride a bicycle that most other children move through. They are highly perfectionistic, and prefer to show others their finished products rather than their growing pains (Keirsey & Bates, 1978).

In parenting introverts, it is important to respect their natural mode of being in the world. Understanding their needs for privacy, solitude, and reflection are essential. If possible, they should not be asked to share a bedroom with an extraverted sibling! Care should be taken to discipline them privately, to avoid humiliating them. When learning new activities, they need to be given time to observe and to practice privately until they are comfortable that they can perform the activities well. Computers are useful educational tools since they maintain the child's privacy during the learning process.

Some introverted children are perfect at school and at other people's homes, and tantrum-prone at home. Parents need to know that this behavior is not due to bad parenting. On the contrary, an introverted child frequently will show negative emotions only to the individual with whom he or she is closest. The closest parent actually provides an escape valve for tensions built up in a child trying to be flawless out in the world. Without this escape valve at home, the child could be headed for serious depression. This does not mean, however, that the beloved parent must always accept the brunt of the child's frustrations. Many parents find sending their children to their rooms for the duration of their tantrums an effective means of dealing with them.

Parents should not be overly concerned if their children are introverts, but should bear in mind that, in adult life, there are many advantages to introversion. Introverts tend to have higher grades in college (Myers, 1962) since they are less distracted by their social life. Many eminent individuals needed long periods of solitude during their most creative periods (Albert, 1978), indicating their introverted temperaments. It may be that the type of public risk-taking behavior regarded as characteristic of the creative personality fits only the creative extravert and overlooks the introvert, whose creativity is a more private affair. Introverts also appear to have advantages in the reflective tasks involved in personality integration, since they are less affected by the values and attitudes of others (Jung, 1938). As they are a minority in our society, most introverts have had to develop some extraverted behaviors in order to cope, but extraverts rarely are called upon to develop the introverted parts of their personalities. Although there is no question that extraversion is advantageous in childhood and young adulthood, the full integration of the personality depends on the development of all aspects of the self, and the introvert may be better prepared for this task than the extravert during the second half of the life cycle.

Creator Parents vs. Responsive Parenting

Today, we face the Superbaby phenomenon, in which many parents in the professional class want to ensure that their children have every advantage in the competition of life by enrolling them as infants in every class imaginable. They believe they can *create* a gifted child from scratch, like a yuppie pasta, and have, therefore, been given the name, "creator parents."

Fortunately, most of the parents of gifted children with whom I have worked over the years are not motivated by this goal. They usually discover their children to be advanced, and then wonder how they should respond to this advancement. They recognize that their children are naturally developing more rapidly than others in the neighborhood: sitting up, walking, talking, reading earlier, and asking more sophisticated, complex questions. This atypical developmental pattern causes the parents some level of anxiety. They ask each other, "Are we doing the right thing?" "Should we be doing something more?" They are genuinely concerned that their children might be misfits or unhappy in school. Their natural tendencies are to respond with delight to their children's own natural developmental schedules and not pushing or molding, just providing the next step as the children seem ready.

By contrast, creator parents use their children as a means of enhancing their own egos. They push their children to do everything early to make themselves feel more successful. The case study of William Sidis, poignantly described by Montour (1977), reveals the tragic consequences that can result from this misuse of childhood. Miller (1981) also warns against the dangers of usurping the child's sense of Self to create a parent-pleasing, performing child. Miller, however, makes the phenomenon appear so widespread as to be nearly inevitable in childrearing. My own professional experience has led me to conclude that these insecure, competitive adults are relatively rare among the community of parents of gifted children. Yet, they leave such an indelible negative impression that many healthy, responsive parents are afraid of teaching or accelerating their children for fear of being regarded in people's minds as creator parents.

Many parents have apologized to me because their children learned to read at the age of 4. They are quick to assure me that they are not responsible: "I didn't teach her, honestly." I have to re-assure them that it is perfectly all right if they did, just as long as they did not pressure the child to acquire skills prematurely. Children have different developmental schedules: some gifted children are ready to read at 3 and others should not begin reading until 9. We have known this for a long time from theories of child development; yet, the common message conveyed to parents is that there is only one ideal time for children to begin to read, at age 6 when reading is introduced in the first grade.

It is important for parents to realize that they are their children's first educators, and that they cannot leave the whole responsibility to the schools. The most powerful influence on the child's future is the home (Goertzel & Goertzel, 1962; Hobbs, 1975; Roedell, Jackson, & Robinson, 1980; White & Watts, 1973) and those adults who have been most successful were taught in the home prior to their formal education (Bloom, 1985; Goertzel & Goertzel, 1962). Parents should therefore be urged to take an active role in supporting the development of their children's talents. An important part of this role is knowing how to encourage and guide without exerting pressure. High expectations and encouragement to do one's best are necessary to success; pressure is not necessary and may actually interfere with achievement.

The difference between the creator parent and the responsive parent is in the degree of emphasis on the child's performance. The creator parent wants performance at all costs, even perhaps at the cost of the child's emotional well-being. The responsive parent conveys to the child that he or she is loved regardless of performance, and that the adventure of risk-taking is more important than success. All children need such assurance of unconditional acceptance from their parents if they are to actualize their potential.

GUIDELINES FOR PARENTING

When gifted high school students were asked to comment on the most valued gifts they received from their parents (American Association for Gifted Children, 1978), several common themes emerged: warmth and affection, respect, honesty, support for their interests, opportunities to develop independence, understanding of their emotional needs, and stimulating home lives.

Parental support is actualized through the provision of an enriching family life which includes exposure to a wide variety of activities and early opportunities to develop special talents and interests. Some abilities, such as gymnastics, ballet, and playing musical instruments, need to be fostered well before school age in order for the full potential of these abilities to be actualized (Bloom, 1985). A rich family life also involves shared meals with lively discussions and humor; times to work and play together; exposure to cultural activities, such as museums, art exhibits, symphonies, theater, dance recitals; family trips; and shared family interests, such as singing, playing musical instruments, sports, computer programming, preparing meals together, storytelling, playing chess and word games, building models, gardening or redecorating.

The following guidelines are an abbreviated version of a set of ideas contained in a chapter on parenting gifted children, from *Gifted Education: A Developmental Approach* (Silverman, in preparation-a).

1. Talk with them in an adult manner, but do not "adultize" them. Do not expect them to be miniature adults.
2. Arrange private times with each child at regular and frequent intervals, so that he or she does not always have to compete for attention.
3. Set appropriate boundaries so that adults have "adult-time" to refresh.
4. Read aloud to them, even after they are old enough to read to themselves.
5. Praise them for taking risks rather than for successful accomplishments. This enables them to better cope with failures.
6. Reason with them rather than setting down arbitrary rules. Give them opportunities to make choices. Appeal to their growing sense of fairness.

7. Discipline them privately rather than publicly.
8. Avoid sarcasm.
9. Avoid comparison; it invites competition.
10. Give them responsibilities as early as possible, gradually increasing the size of the tasks as they are ready to assume them.
11. Let them discover their own ways of doing things. Allow them to make mistakes. Avoid criticism or unnecessary corrections which might embarrass them.
12. Nurture their creativity. Encourage them to develop their imaginations and to discuss their imaginary companions. Invent visualization games and fantasies with them.
13. Provide opportunities for them to interact often with other gifted children, older children, and stimulating adults.
14. Help them learn social skills of enhancing others' self-esteem.
15. Help them gain confidence in their own perceptions, even when they differ from other people's.
16. Take time to listen to them.
17. Be open to their questions. Don't think you have to know all the answers. Instead, ask, "What do you think?" Encourage self-evaluation.
18. Do not try to create extraverts out of introverts.
19. Accept that some children will have narrow interests and others, broad interests. The world needs both types.
20. Hold family councils so that they will have an opportunity to participate in shared decision-making.
21. Don't expect that their lives will replicate the parent's. Each child is unique.
22. Don't overschedule them with activities. Allow them time to think, play, daydream and to be children.
23. Do not cater to their every whim and ask nothing in return. Teach them how to give.
24. Recognize them for being instead of for doing.
25. Keep parental expectations realistic.
26. Encourage their autonomy.
27. Do not attempt to inhibit their perfectionism or sensitivity.
28. Do not encourage them to hide their abilities.
29. Be their advocates. Support their right to be themselves.
30. Above all, enjoy them.

Evaluating Program Options
for Young Gifted Children

Margie Kitano, PhD

ABSTRACT. Young gifted children display a wide range of individual differences with regard to needs, interests, and abilities. As a result, no single program or method may be appropriate for all young gifted children. In considering placement options for a given child, parents and educators should attempt to maximize the match between program characteristics and the individual child's needs. Program features to consider include the population served (general population or gifted only), administrative arrangement (enrichment and/or acceleration), goals (academic and/or social), and degree of structure or flexibility. Important child characteristics include degree of advancement, areas of advancement, tolerance for individual differences, adaptability, and social-emotional maturity. In addition to providing the most appropriate match for a child, effective early childhood programs also provide a clearly established philosophy, goals, management plan, monitoring system, specialized activities and materials, opportunities for individualization, parent involvement, and continuity with other programs.

One question parents of young gifted children frequently ask of professional educators concerns the "best" program for their children. The dilemma in responding to this question stems from the fact that the "best" program for a given child depends on that child's particular needs. Gifted children of the same chronological age may vary in pattern of strengths and weakenesses (e.g., levels of creativity, verbal or analytical intelligence), talent areas (e.g., music or mathematics), interests (e.g., quilting or astronomy), socioemotional maturity, and educational experiences. With the range of characteristics, abilities, and needs presented by gifted children, no single program may be the most appropriate for all.

Margie Kitano is Head of the Department of Special Education/Communication Disorders at New Mexico State University and is Director of the New Mexico State University Preschool for the Gifted. She is co-author with Darrell Kirby of a promising new text released early in 1986 by Little, Brown and Company, *Gifted Education: A Comprehensive View.*

89

How, then, can parents make intelligent decisions, and educators make valid recommendations, about the most appropriate placement or program for a certain child? Given a choice among several high quality programs, the major consideration hinges on the match or degree of "fit" between the characteristics of the program and the child's special needs. The purpose of this article is to provide guidelines for assessing the characteristics of programs and the extent to which they are appropriate for young gifted children.

The quality of teachers constitutes the most important feature of any educational program. Teachers of gifted young children should have training and experience in gifted education and child development, and provide a positive, motivating, well-managed environment. Parents generally have well-defined ideas about the types of teachers that will motivate their individual children to participate and excel in school. Hence, while recognizing the central role of teacher characteristics in determining program effectiveness, this article focuses on additional information that parents and educators may find helpful in selecting from program *options* frequently available for young gifted children. For example, should a given child be placed in a program which offers: (a) homogeneous or heterogeneous grouping? (b) enrichment or acceleration? (c) academic or social emphases? and (d) open or structured curricula and methods? Information about the strengths and weaknesses of the various program options can help parents and educators make informed decisions.

HOMOGENEOUS AND HETEROGENEOUS GROUPING

Homogeneous grouping refers to the bringing together of children who meet some established set of criteria for inclusion. Special programs for gifted students typically are designed to serve gifted children exclusively; all children selected for the program meet the designated standards for inclusion. In contrast, programs designed for heterogeneous groups generally include children representing a broad scope of ability levels within a specific age group, sometimes ranging from low-average to superior aptitude for learning.

Each type of program has distinctive features and effects. Grouping gifted children together permits teachers to teach higher-level curriculum content and to more consistently use appropriate instructional methods. Second, gifted children in self-contained, homogeneous classrooms continuously challenge each other intellectually and are not held back while the teacher accommodates the needs of slower learners. Third, gifted children who are accustomed to being ''stars'' in heterogeneous settings learn to recognize that there are others whose talents may be equal or superior to their own. On the other hand, gifted children integrated with their nongifted peers have the advantage of learning to interact with a broader range of individuals and to understand that some children do not learn as quickly as themselves. While some experts argue that homogeneous grouping provides gifted children with a more realistic view of their abilities, it can be countered that heterogeneous grouping provides an experience more similar to the real world outside of and beyond formal schooling.

The choice between homogeneous and heterogeneous grouping depends on the individual child's needs, particularly with regard to the individual child's self-concept. Most of the literature on the self-concepts of gifted children indicates that, as a group, gifted children manifest more positive self-concepts than nongifted children (Kelly & Colangelo, 1984; Lehman & Erdwins, 1981). Several studies have suggested, though, that gifted children's self-concepts may become more negative when they are placed in homogeneous settings where they compare themselves to children of equal or greater ability (Coleman & Fults, 1982, 1985). Nonetheless, gifted children placed in homogeneous settings continue to report generally more positive self-concepts than do children in the nongifted population.

It is important to note that most self-concept research has been conducted with upper-elementary or secondary-age gifted children and it is unclear whether the findings can be generalized to younger gifted children, especially those who have not had previous school experience. Nevertheless, the available studies do suggest that children who have more fragile self-concepts tend to benefit most from being placed in heterogeneous settings. One child known by the author became extremely frustrated by her average status in a preschool for gifted children. She became verbally and physically aggressive in her efforts to regain the attention that she had received in her former setting, a regular community nursery program.

Children who demonstrate very positive self-concepts, strong egos, and a tendency toward impatience with others of lesser ability may be more appropriately placed in a homogeneous group of students, which is apt to be more humbling as well as more challenging. For example, one child encountered by the author berated his nongifted peers for making "dumb" spelling errors. His intolerance of slower children and obvious need for faster pacing, more indepth experiences, and rigorous intellectual competition rendered him a prime candidate for a homogeneous setting.

Some schools offer "pull-out" programs for young gifted children which combine the advantages of both types of grouping. Here, gifted children are placed, sometimes in clusters, within the regular grade-appropriate, heterogeneous classroom and are "pulled out" for special services. Pull-out programs bring gifted children together at regularly scheduled intervals (e.g., one hour a day or one day a week) for special projects or curricula. When there is a cluster grouping of gifted students in regular classrooms, those teachers bring the gifted children together for appropriate instruction in specific areas of the curriculum, such as reading, mathematics, or science.

In addition to the child's needs for interacting with gifted or nongifted peers, two other points merit consideration in making a decision about the appropriate grouping for a child. First, homogeneous grouping of gifted children does not automatically result in the most effective, appropriate instruction. A program's designation as a "gifted" program does not guarantee that the program is more appropriate for or beneficial to gifted children than alternatives might be. All too often parents and teachers are satisfied with a child's acceptance into a "gifted" program, making the assumption that, because the child is gifted and the program was ostensibly designed for gifted students, the match is good. Rather, any type of grouping must be accompanied by appropriate modifications in the instructional process and the content of the curriculum. Second, within homogeneous programs, individualization is still required in order to accommodate the wide range of interests and abilities and the diverse special needs within the gifted group.

ACCELERATION AND ENRICHMENT

Simply stated, *acceleration* moves children vertically through the regular curriculum at a faster pace than is typical. The child may remain in the age-appropriate grouping but progress to curriculum levels designated for higher grades (curriculum acceleration) or the child may "skip" one or more grades to learn with older children (grade acceleration). *Enrichment* refers to programs that retain children in their regular grade level but expand the curriculum content by adding depth to the topics covered, by incorporating higher level and creative thinking processes, and/or by requiring different products. The issue for both parents and teachers is related to the potential effects of grade acceleration on specific children. Generally all agree that appropriate modifications for gifted children placed in regular grade-level classrooms must include both curriculum enrichment and acceleration. Again, each programming option has advantages and disadvantages depending on the individual child's needs.

Acceleration enables children to complete the standard school curriculum in less time than is usual. Modes of acceleration for gifted young children include early entrance to kindergarten or first grade, grade skipping, part-time grade skipping, and combined classes. Part-time grade skipping may be appropriate for children who demonstrate superiority only in one or a few areas. For example, a 5-year-old who reads on the second grade level may attend a second grade classroom for reading but remain in kindergarten for socialization. Combined classes bring together in one classroom children from two or more grade levels, such as first and second grades. This setting permits younger children to interact socially with older children and to be grouped flexibly for more advanced instruction in subjects related to specific academic giftedness while learning with younger children in other curriculum areas.

Many parents and teachers question the appropriateness of grade acceleration for young gifted children because of concerns regarding their social and emotional growth, need for interaction with chronological-age peers, and physical and motor immaturity for successful participation in an advanced placement. Yet, research conducted over the last 50 years clearly supports the efficacy of grade acceleration for some or many gifted students. As a group, accelerated children have evidenced equal or better achievement and social adjustment compared to children of equal ability who were not accelerated (Braga, 1971; Getzels & Dillon, 1973; Paulus, 1984). In a follow-up study of sixth to eighth grade children permitted early entrance to kindergarten (Alexander & Skinner, 1980), ten of eleven maintained A or A/B grade point averages throughout their school history. All eleven participated in a wide range of extracurricular activities. Although two students indicated that their younger age excluded them from some activities, these comments were far outweighed by their positive remarks.

Parents have reported several advantages to grade acceleration, including avoiding boredom and learning to work to remain in the upper portion of the class when learning previously had come too easily. It appears that most gifted children understand and adjust to the realities of age and size differences. It is important to compare these relatively minor inconveniences with the social-emotional problems that can emerge when very advanced children are held back in the regular grade levels and forced to wait for their peers to "catch up."

Enrichment refers to meeting gifted children's needs through broadening, deepening, or expanding the regular curriculum. While the term "enrichment" is often used to designate provisions of differentiated learning experiences for gifted children within the regular (heterogeneous) classroom, it also can characterize homogeneous programs designed for the gifted. Effective enrichment programs provide a well-articulated curriculum that includes activities which require higher-level cognitive processing, indepth investigation or curriculum content, a wider range of content, and/or challenging modes of communication.

The efficacy of enrichment has not been clearly determined due to the variability in the types and quality of programs given this designation. Enrichment programs of high quality meet gifted children's interests and needs while maintaining them in the regular program with their chronological-age peers. Although conceptually sound, appropriate enrichment is difficult to implement given large heterogeneous classrooms with one teacher. Assurance of teacher effectiveness with gifted children and individualization to meet the special needs of individuals are critical factors in selecting the enrichment option.

Two major factors are important in determining whether acceleration or enrichment constitutes the better option for a given gifted child. First, the child's characteristics and needs should be evaluated with regard to (a) degree of advancement in relation to classmates, (b) areas of advanced achievement, (c) tendency for boredom, and (d) social-emotional as well as physical maturity. Early admission and grade skipping may be mandatory for meeting the needs of highly gifted students who are extremely advanced in mastery of academic content. For a child, however, who is advanced in only one or two specific areas of achievement such as reading, mathematics, or computer programming, part-time acceleration may be more appropriate. Gifted children who become intensely frustrated by repetition and slower pacing also constitute candidates for grade acceleration. Finally, academically advanced children who lack independence and initiative, adequate social interaction skills, and/or physical development sufficient for completing written assignments and for successful participation in socially-valued activities (e.g., games) may benefit more from part-time than full-time acceleration.

Each child's particular constellation of characteristics must be considered in determining placement options. For examle, one 5-year-old boy in the author's experience demonstrated advanced achievement in all areas, including social maturity, suggesting the appropriateness of early entrance to first grade. An additional area of giftedness for him, however, was adaptability. He thoroughly enjoyed his classmates and found something new and fascinating in any topic or activity, novel or old, presented by the teacher. His parents decided that the pressure of competing with older children in a higher grade might diminish his enthusiasm; the author concurred.

A second factor in considering the option of acceleration is the continuity of services. Acceleration, by definition, permits the child to move through the regular curriculum at a more rapid pace. Thus, after mastering the regular curriculum, the child is left with extra time. For example, the advanced reader may finish the second grade reading curriculum in kindergarten through part-time placement in the second grade just for reading. The advantage of such acceleration decreases if the child's subsequent teachers or administrators do not provide options for continuing the child's progress in reading. Similarly, the child who skips grades at a rapid pace may finish the twelfth grade curriculum without enough credits to receive a high school diploma unless the district has made special provisions for awarding credit. The advantage of acceleration is diminished unless specific provisions are made to continue the acceleration or to make use of extra time created through accelerated programming, such as special seminars or mentorships.

ACADEMIC AND SOCIAL EMPHASES

While programs for young gifted children vary in their stated goals and objectives, most of these programs have in common emphases on (a) basic skill development (language, reading, motor skills, quantitative concepts); (b) acquisition of disciplinary knowledge (social studies, science); (c) development of thinking skills (problem solving, creativity); and (d) social/affective development (positive attitudes toward school, self, and peers, and adequate social competence). Some programs additionally provide opportunities for the development of special talents (e.g., music, art), interests, or a second language. Goals for a given program are not empirically derived, but rather philosophically determined. The selection of goals involves answering the values question: what should young gifted children know and do? After a program has determined its goals, time limitations often require selective emphases on certain ones. For example, most programs for gifted preschool-age children meet only a few hours a day or for only a few days per week. The major question about goals in selecting a program for a young gifted child concerns the child's relative needs for social development and basic academic achievement (reading, writing, arithmetic).

Our experience over the last four years at the New Mexico State University Preschool for the Gifted indicates that parents differ in their expectations regarding program goals. Some parents emphasize social development experiences that will enable their children to overcome shyness and establish friendships. Others expect their children to make substantial advances in reading, writing, and mathemtics skills. Although a preschool program for gifted children undoubtedly includes goals of both social and academic development, parents will want to select one with an emphasis that matches their expectations and goals for their child.

Evaluation studies of individual preschool programs (Hanninen, 1984; Karnes, Shwedel, & Lewis, 1983a, 1983b; VanTassal-Baska, Schuler, & Lipschutz, 1982) clearly indicate that young gifted children make academic gains in programs designed to achieve this end. That bright children can advance academically through special preschool programs is hardly surprising. Rather, the question is: Because gifted children can acquire knowledge and skills at an earlier age than their nongifted peers, should early acquisition of knowledge be a major program goal? Moreover, many gifted children enter preschool programs already achieving two years or more above their chronological age expectancy level. The question then becomes whether preschool programs for the gifted should focus on increasing gifted young children's already advanced academic skills. For what purpose should advanced achievement be emphasized?

Our work at the NMSU Preschool for the Gifted (Kitano, 1985b) suggests a greater need for the development of prosocial motivation and a lesser need for academic pressure. We find that some gifted children enter preschool possessing mature social skills (e.g., greeting others, inviting others to play) but choose not to apply these skills (Kitano, 1985a). For example, a child demonstrates in one situation the ability to share and include others in play. In another situation, the same child hoards the materials and refuses to let others play, thus opting in this situation not to use his or her earlier demonstrated positive social skills. In other words, the child's failure to share is not due to a lack of social skills, but rather to lack of motivation or perception of the need to use these skills.

Moreover, an ethnographic study (Kitano, 1985a) of children in the NMSU program suggested that children as young as 3 and 4 years of age begin schooling with a competitive motive to be "the best" or "the first." Although some might argue that a competitive spirit is required for survival in the real world, one might question the appropriateness of competitive pressure at an early age. If gifted children become the leaders of the future, the values of teamwork, appreciation of individual differences, empathy, and humanistic understanding appear to be more critical attributes. Roedell (1985) noted that gifted young children's mature vocabularies and ideas, and frequently uneven development, make them vulnerable to social isolation; hence, curricula emphasizing the development of social competence become of critical value to gifted preschool-age children.

Accelerated academic learning, especially in reading, mathematics, and science, is important for children who are developmentally ready to advance in these areas, who display interest and motivation, and who would otherwise be bored. Parents who insist that their gifted children be taught to read, write, and compute at an early age in the absence of these developmental and motivational factors should reflect on their motives and the potential consequences of placing their children in such a program. For example, some parents request advanced learning so that the child can enter first grade at an early age. Again, for what purpose?

Part of the parent emphasis on academic learning may be rooted in the erroneous assumptions that (a) children are not gifted unless they read by age 5, and (b) children who read by age 5 or earlier are gifted. In fact, Terman's early studies (1926) on middle-class intellectually gifted children and more recent investigations (Cassidy & Vukelich, 1980) indicate that fewer than half of the identified gifted children read before entering kindergarten. Factors which affect early reading skill acquisition include opportunities for reading, parent and child interest in reading, and physical maturity. Some evidence (Moore, Moon, & Moore, 1972) suggest that visual and auditory systems necessary for reading may mature in some children as late as age 7 or 8.

Again, the selection of goals and the relative emphasis on each in the program is a values decision and must be made with respect to the individual child's needs. In general, two points should be considered. First, children who express a desire to advance academically and who are developmentally ready must be accommodated. Children who show no interest in advancing beyond their chronological age expectancy level and/or who are not developmentally ready should not be pressured to achieve, but should be given opportunities to learn through activities which stimulate their advanced interests and abilities. Second, all programs should emphasize the development of social consciousness and competence so that gifted children learn to apply their skills and knowledge in directions beneficial to themselves and others.

CURRICULUM AND METHODS

A number of different models for curriculum and program planning have been applied to preschool programs for the gifted: Bloom's Taxonomy (Bailey & Leonard, 1977), Open Classroom (Karnes, Kemp, & Williams, 1983), Enrichment Triad Model (Karnes, Kemp, & Williams, 1983), Structure of Intellect (Karnes, Kemp, & Williams, 1983), Multiple Talent Approach (Schlichter, 1985), Unit Approach (Kitano & Kirby, in press-b). Space limitations preclude a comparison of each model. Rather, several issues are raised which can help parents determine whether a given program's model for curriculum and program planning is appropriate for their child.

1. *Are program goals clearly specified?* One of the first questions that should be asked about a program is its goals for the children. Well-defined goals help parents determine whether the program matches the child's needs. Program staff can also explain how these goals are translated into daily activities.

2. *How effective has the program been in accomplishing its goals?* A program which has been in existence for several years

should be able to provide data indicating its efficacy. For example, the program may reassess children at the end of the year to measure gains. Parents may be asked to respond to questionnaires to ascertain their perceptions of their child's growth. These data should be used to continually monitor and modify the program.

3. *Does the program provide continuity with other programs?* Parents need to know what programs are available for their children after they complete the current one. For example, if the child attends a special preschool for gifted 4-year-olds and "graduates" to a public school kindergarten, (a) will the child's program continue into the kindergarten? and (b) will support be provided to facilitate the transition? In other words, parents need information concerning opportunities available to continue appropriate enrichment and accelerated learning beyond the preschool program. Many programs for young gifted children have established close working relationships with school programs to ensure articulation and to ease the child's transition.

4. *Who determines the curriculum?* Some programs permit children's interests to determine what is taught. For example, large portions of time may be allocated to individual projects selected by the child (e.g., model building, collecting, clay modeling) with the teacher providing resources and guidance. At the other extreme are programs which have a predetermined curriculum with little deviation from planned activities. Still other programs provide a range of teacher-selected activities which permit children to discover interests and later pursue self-selected projects related to one interest area. Some children enter school with definite interests which they expect to pursue. Others display no particular interests and prefer teacher-structured activities. In selecting a program, parents and educators should consider the child's need for structure/flexibility, the child's desire to pursue specific interests, and the program's policies regarding use of parent input in determining what is taught. In sum, parents will want to select a program which best suits their philosophy regarding how the curriculum is determined and the degree of structure or flexibility with which it is provided.

5. *Does the program help children learn how to learn?* Many gifted children easily acquire facts and knowledge, frequently through incidental learning. Because they have many opportunities throughout the day to acquire facts, school programs for young gifted children might be better aimed at teaching them how to discover and use information. Goals should include practice in processing academic

and social information through activities designed to encourage problem solving, creativity, leadership, motivation, responsibility, and independent functioning. The challenging program will also teach children to learn from mistakes, which are a natural part of learning.

   6. *How does the program provide for individual child needs?* Where individualization is a program feature, program staff can explain the process by which individualization occurs in the classroom. For example, some programs assess children individually to determine what they can and cannot do with respect to specific skill areas (e.g., work learning letters, colors, and number recognition). Based on the assessment data, staff and parents jointly design an individualized educational plan which will establish objectives and guide instructional activities for the child. The plan may incorporate the child's interests and parents' goals for the child. Teachers then implement the individual plans through grouping, one-on-one instruction, or projects.

SUMMARY AND CONCLUSIONS

   The foregoing discussion of program options urges parents and educators to evaluate the characteristics of a given program in terms of the specific needs of their gifted child. No single model or method has been demonstrated as most effective for all gifted children. Rather, a careful match must be made between the particular program's characteristics and the particular child's needs. Several general criteria for evaluating program characteristics and quality can be summarized from the options discussed. A program for gifted young children should offer:

1. a clear statement of philosophy, purpose, and goals;
2. a clear management plan (e.g., homogeneous or heterogeneous grouping, acceleration or enrichment) consistent with program philosophy and goals;
3. activities and materials which enable the goals to be accomplished;
4. specific provisions for individualization of curriculum and instruction;
5. a system for regular monitoring of children's growth with respect to specific goals for affective and cognitive development;

6. opportunities for parent involvement in developing objectives for the child;
7. specific provisions for ensuring program continuity with other programs; and
8. teachers effective with gifted students.

The assessment of a child's needs should consider his/her self-concept; tolerance for bordeom; level and type of interests, degree of advancement in the development of specific skills and knowledge of content areas; areas of less advancement or weakness; socio-emotional maturity; reaction to pressure for achievement, including competitiveness among peers; and empathy for others. Clearly, the "best" program for a young gifted child is the one most consistent with his or her needs.

PART IV:
SPECIAL NEEDS
AND EDUCATIONAL ISSUES

Introduction

A fundamental premise of the authors is that the early educational experiences of gifted children will critically influence the extent to which children with exceptionally high intellectual potential become high achievers or underachievers. The specific needs of gifted children make them vulnerable to underachievement if appropriate educational opportunities are not provided. The rationale for early education for gifted children is grounded in prevention of the development of undesirable attitudes and patterns of underachievement.

Two of the most persuasive examples of the powerfully positive effects of appropriate guidance and educational intervention during the early years are the topics of the articles in this section. In the first article, Carolyn Callahan reports research findings regarding the potentially negative effects of differential treatment of young boys and girls that ultimately affects the motivation and achievement of gifted females. In the second article, the powerful effects of schooling in the primary grades are described through the example of the special Cupertino, California intervention program which successfully reversed patterns of school failure in highly gifted children. These articles, we believe, contribute significantly to a defensible rationale for a policy requiring gifted education programs to be provided in the first years of school, and guide both parents and teachers to more effective interaction with gifted youngsters of both sexes.

103

The Special Needs
of Gifted Girls

Carolyn M. Callahan, PhD

ABSTRACT. The differential adult achievement level of males and females has been widely noted and lamented. This article examines intellectual, educational, social and personality factors affecting the achievement of the gifted female during the very early years. Potential influences of differential achievement from parental and teacher behaviors, the media, toys and play are described and strategies for nurturing behaviors and attitudes more conducive to adult achievement are discussed.

Before you begin reading this article, please take a piece of paper and attempt these three tasks:

1. List five males who have made significant contributions to science; then, name five females who have made significant contributions to science.
2. List five male classical composers and five female classical composers.
3. List five males who have made significant contributions to the art world, and five females who have made significant contributions to the art world.

How did you do? Most people have little trouble with the first part of each task, but very few individuals can actually complete the tasks. Our struggle to identify females who have been recognized as significant contributors in the arts, the sciences, and other professions is testimony to the underachievement of gifted females—the issue to be addressed in the text which follows.

Carolyn M. Callahan is Associate Professor and Director of the Summer Enrichment Program at the University of Virginia, and has served in the presidency of the Association for the Gifted (TAG), a division of the Council for Exceptional Children (CEC). Dr. Callahan has contributed numerous publications on the topics of evaluation and gender differences relative to gifted education.

WHAT IS THE PROBLEM?

One of the most significant movements during the past three decades has been the women's movement. Widespread attention and political action have focused on the lack of opportunity for equal education, equal access to jobs, comparable salaries and compensation, and equal social and political rights. At the same time, there has been increasing concern about the gifted child and that child's needs and educational rights. Interestingly, the two areas are in many ways more closely tied than one might expect at first glance. For how can we expect the gifted woman to be able to take advantage of opportunities if she has not developed the skills, the confidence, and the motivation to pursue goals which are commensurate with her abilities? The problem of which we are becoming increasingly aware is the vulnerability of gifted females to patterns of significant underachievement.

The failure of gifted women to realize their potential for high achievement and leadership often is not recognized until those individuals reach adolescence or adulthood, but the practices that inhibit the development of that potential can be traced as far back as the practices and attitudes of parents toward newborn infants and to the earliest educational programs (i.e., preschool and the kindergarten-primary grades). That is to say, the special needs of gifted females must be addressed early and systematically if we are to expect that adolescent and adult gifted women will achieve at the same levels and with the same consistency as gifted men. In order to create the conditions which will maximize the gifted girl's potential, it is important that we understand the factors which distinguish gifted females from gifted males, that we identify the causes of underachievement in females, and that we actively counter the forces which inhibit fulfillment of exceptional potential.

WHAT DIFFERENCES ACTUALLY EXIST?

Regardless of sex, profession, educational level or bias, everyone seems to agree that the long-term or adult achievement of males surpasses that of females in every area of professional accomplishment, despite an almost universal identification of males as underachievers in elementary school (Shaw & McCuen, 1960; Whitmore, 1980); despite the finding that higher grades are achieved by females throughout elementary, high school, and college (Achenbach, 1970;

Coleman, 1961; Davis, 1964); and despite the finding that males were more likely than females to have total grade point averages and grades in both English and mathematics that were lower than might be predicted by their scores on standardized tests of ability (Stockard & Wood, 1984). What is the origin of these differences in adult accomplishment? What factors contribute to the continued dominance of males in professional areas?

Differences in Cognitive Abilities and Achievement

Standardized tests of intelligence do not offer any evidence of sex differences in ability largely because any items found to discriminate between the sexes are eliminated as the tests are developed. It is, therefore, necessary to look to tests of specific aptitudes to determine whether there are specific ability areas in which males and females differ. Traditional views of male and female abilities, both from within the professional field of education and from society at large, have long attributed greater verbal ability to females and greater mathematical, spatial reasoning and scientific ability to males, at least within school settings. The most comprehensive summary of studies on differences between the sexes (Maccoby & Jacklin, 1974) concluded that there are no differences in cognitive abilities prior to the onset of adolescence and that, after the onset of adolescence, females outscore males in measure of verbal ability and males outscore females in the areas of quantitative and spatial ability.

The conclusions of Benbow and Stanley (1980) relative to mathematical ability among gifted students are congruent with those of Maccoby and Jacklin. However, recent reviews of the data have raised questions about the significance and meaningfulness of the differences (Hyde, 1981; Caplan, MacPherson, & Tobin, 1985), about the definition of spatial abilities (Caplan et al., 1985), about the validity of the studies, and about sex bias within the instruments used in the studies (Hyde, 1981; Naditch, 1976). Finally, numerous studies have demonstrated that brief instructions, in areas where supposed differences in ability exist, have been successful in eradicating those differences (Conner, Shackman, & Serbin, 1978; Goldstein & Chance, 1965; Johnson, 1976; Tobin, 1982). It thus seems fair to conclude that differences in cognitive abilities are doubtful and, even if they do exist, they are not sufficiently large to account for the differences in adult achievement.

Differences in Cognitive Style and Personality

Although actual sex differences in mathematical ability and spatial reasoning ability are debatable, Hyde (1981) argues that even if we accept the largest reported differences in those areas, the high ratio of male Noble prize award winners to female winners still should not be nearly as large as it is. Furthermore, there have never been any ability differences which can account for the large discrepancy between the number of male and female Pulitzer Prize winners. If gender differences in cognitive abilities do not account for the large discrepancies in achievement by the sexes, then we must look to other traits which can explain the differences.

Personality Differences

Much research has been done on cognitive styles and personality traits which appear related to success and outstanding achievement. One trait which appears to be closely related to achievement, and on which males and females differ significantly, is the way in which people offer explanations for success or failure at a task. Studies by Dweck and her colleagues found that bright girls tend to attribute their success to luck or chance factors and their failures to personality flaws, whereas boys attribute their success to their ability and their failures to chance (Licht & Dweck, 1984). Deaux and Farris (1977) found that when a task was labelled masculine, men expected to do better, evaluated their performance more favorably (even though they had performed at the same level as women), claimed more ability, and attributed less to luck. When the task was labelled feminine, there were few differences in how sexes evaluated their performance.

In a review of similar investigations, Deaux (1984) concluded that when expectations for success differ (with women predicting lower performance for themselves on masculine tasks), women will tend to exhibit lower performance. She also reported that female performance is more highly related to expectation levels of others in the environment. Even more detrimental to the ultimate success of females is a learned belief that they are less capable than males and the formation of a set of lower expectations for success. These traits are not traits which manifest themselves only in the later years of the developmental process. Crandall, Katkovsky, and Preston (1962) found that first-grade girls already had lower expectations for success on a new learning task *and* that the higher the boys' IQ, the greater his expectations for success while the exact opposite was true for girls. Parsons, Ruble, Hodges, and Small (1976) similarly reported that girls appear to have lower perceptions of their competence relative to boys as early as kindergarten.

In a different vein, Hoffman (1972) suggests that females have high needs for affiliation which may at times hinder achievement. In her summary of the research literature, she points out that "even at preschool age girls have different orientations toward intellectual tasks than do boys. Little girls want to please; they work for love and approval; if bright, they underestimate their competence. Little boys show more task involvement, more confidence . . . . Girls have more anxiety than boys and the anxiety they have is more dysfunctional to their performance" (p. 130). Hoffman also points out that women who indicate fear of success demonstrate poorer performance in a competitive task than when they perform that same task alone.

In addition, children develop well-defined conceptions of "boy traits" and "girl traits" as early as the primary grades. For example, boys tend to perceive boldness as positively correlated with male popularity while girls perceive it as negatively correlated with female popularity (Tuddenham, 1952). Problem solving also has been shown to be directly related to sex role stereotyping, with androgynous personality types performing equally well on all tasks regardless of the type of cue given. Masculine types performed best when no cues were given as to sex role appropriateness and feminine types performed best when cues were available (Ho, 1981). The origins of these differences may well relate to early experiences, toys, and modelling which will be discussed at a later point.

Another way in which personality and values seem to affect the aspirations and achievement of gifted girls is in the lack of variability manifested on nearly all measures of personality traits. That is, women tend not to score at the extreme high or low of any distribution (Callahan, 1979). One explanation may be that girls are motivationally influenced most by a desire to conform and thus they often fail to demonstrate exceptional characteristics because of a fear of rejection. Gilligan (1982) notes that conformity is prized and heavily reinforced by parents, teachers, and friends of the young female.

Cognitive Style

Researchers who have studied cognitive style, or the way in which individuals approach learning and problem solving, have found that men and women differ on a number of dimensions *but* that the difference appears to occur only when presented with tasks identified as male and not when parallel feminine tasks are presented (Deaux, 1984). On masculine-oriented tasks, males were consistently more field independent and analytic in their problem solving. This trait has been linked to the greater spatial reasoning abilities of children and associated with childrearing practices (Callahan, 1979).

In sum, those sex differences which do exist are: (a) limited to the cognitive areas of spatial and mathematical abilities, (b) apparent in some personality areas relating to achievement, (c) not large enough to account for differential rates of achievement, and (d) surprisingly small given the differences in the way the sexes are treated.

ORIGINS OF DIFFERENTIAL ACHIEVEMENT

If differences in achievement are genetically determined, then we are obliged to accept the lower achievement levels of the gifted female (at least until the time when genetic engineering is an option). If the reasons for differental achievement, however, are environmental, then there are many ways we can alter the experiences of children to enhance the full development of their exceptional potential for high achievement. At this point in time, there is no way to be absolutely sure of the proportionate influences of environment and heredity on the ultimate achievement of gifted individuals. There is *considerable* evidence, however, that the different ways in which parents, teachers and the society at large interact with young girls influence the values, attitudes, motivation and personality characteristics related to achievement and behaviors associated with achievement. For example, Caplan et al. (1985) concluded that the 1% to 5% of the variance in spatial and mathematical abilities can "more than adequately be explained by environmental differences . . . Indeed, in view of the dramatic differences in the way sexes are raised, it seems surprising that the sex difference—when it is found—accounts for such a small proportion of the variance" (p. 787). In the following section, major factors or forces that shape the differential achievement of gifted males and females will be described concisely.

Parental and Teacher Influences

Environmental influences begin at birth (if not sooner) and there is a large body of research on cognitive development and social learning which attributes observed sex differences to the development of sex role concepts; to the influence of parents and other adults who treat boys and girls differently from birth onward (Birns, 1976; Frisch, 1977; Fagot, 1973; Smith & Lloyd, 1978); and even to the types of games, and toys and the behaviors encouraged by playing these games or with these toys (O'Brien, Huston, & Risley, 1983). Rubin, Provenzano, and Luria (1974) reported that, even though infant girls tend to be more physically robust, their parents perceive them to be more fragile. Girl babies are touched more gently, their cries answered more frequently, and they are touched or patted more often although boys are actually picked up and handled more frequently and are stimulated more (Garai & Scheinfeld, 1968; Goldberg & Lewis, 1969; Stone & Church, 1973; Hoffman, 1972).

Rubin, Provenzano, and Luria (1974) concluded that "parental sex-typing has already begun its course at the earliest moment in the life of the child" (p. 513). They reported research which found that fathers had different (greater) expectations for sons. Similarly, Lewis (1972) found that parents of infant and toddler boys tend to stress the development of exploratory behavior and independent behavior while parents of girls tend to encourage greater physical proximity to adults. Parents report allowing boys to cross the street by themselves earlier, a greater willingness to allow boys to play with sharp instruments earlier, a willingness to allow boys to play away from home for a long period of time earlier, etc. (Hoffman, 1972). The significance of this differential treatment of young boys and girls is made clear when related to the finding of Kagan and Moss (1962) that maternal protectiveness during the first three years is negatively related to adult achievement for girls. Differential parental interaction with young boys and girls is likely to give messages of greater confidence and competence to males and to give the reverse messages to females.

Other findings which seem to have a direct impact on female development are the tendency of adults to give: (a) a greater amount of feedback (both positive and negative) to males than to females, (b) a greater variety of toys to boys than to girls, (c) more toys to boys which encourage inventiveness and manipulation, and (d) guidance and instruction in different ways to boys and girls (Block, 1981). For example, when told to teach their child how to draw a house with an etch-a-sketch, parents are more likely to demonstrate a strategy to a girl first and then give her the toy, but they allow the boy to begin exploration and then provide suggestions on how to complete the task. Mothers have been shown to hinder their daughters' independence by responding more immediately and positively to their requests for help in solving a task while waiting longer for sons to solve the problem independently (Block, 1981). Girls tend to be discouraged from active involvement and from developing a sense of capability even by the clothes parents choose for them (e.g., little boys have shirts that button in the front; little girls have dresses that button in the back) (Silverman, in press).

Teachers have been observed reinforcing the same differences in male and female behavior. In studying preschool classrooms, Serbin, O'Leary, Kent, and Tonick (1973) concluded that teachers were more likely to respond when boys rather than girls were aggressive, that they used more loud reprimands when scolding boys, gave increased attention to girls when they stayed close by, and *used more directions and instruction when responding to solicitation by boys.* In a study of teaching concept-evaluation problems, girls in the highest achievement group were observed to have received the lowest levels of supportive, ego-enhancing feedback, and to have received the fewest compliments and the most criticism. The Sadkers (1985) reported that boys dominated the classrooms they studied: (a) boys' answers were accepted whether they had raised their hands or not while girls' answers were not accepted unless their hands were raised; (b) boys were called on more often; (c) boys' answers were more often accepted as correct even when they were no more correct than the girls; and (d) boys were more often asked "thinking questions" and girls were more often asked memory questions. The newsletter of Project EFFECT in 1984 reported that one of every three classrooms is segregated by sex, both male and female teachers spend the majority of their instructional time working with male students, and many classrooms have a star student to whom the teacher directs approximately 20 percent of all comments. That student is most often a white male.

Sadly, teachers of the gifted also have attitudes which are detrimental to the development of the gifted female. Cooley, Chauvin, and Karnes (1984) reported that, even though female teachers perceived the possibility of gifted females being in occupations previously closed to women, teachers of both sexes tended to not view gifted females as logical thinkers and to judge gifted male students as better critical thinkers and creative problem-solvers. Male teachers of the gifted tended to judge the gifted female to be more emotional, more high strung, and more gullible than the gifted male.

Television

Although the relative influence of television on children's behavior, values and attitudes has been greatly debated in both the popular press and in the field of social psychology, the fact remains that most children devote a considerable portion of each day to viewing television. The portrayal of males and females in dramatic series, situation comedies and cartoons is likely to influence children's perceptions of appropriate sex role behavior and to shape their idea of sex appropriate behavior. Consider Saturday morning cartoons, for example. The small number of female cartoon characters is shocking and, in those cartoons where they are presnt, the female characters assume only passive or diminutive roles. For example, all of the female characters in the Care Bears are stereotypic in roles and the one female in the Smurf family even has a diminutive name—Smurfette! Only Wonder Woman is seen as an action character and she must rely on magical powers to succeed in problem solving! Cartoons are not alone in their portrayal of the weak female and the problem-solving male. How many women physicians are seen endorsing medical products? How many females portray professionals in situation comedies? Of course, the stereotypic image of males leaves much to be desired, also.

Toys and Play

One of the crucial factors in a child's development is play and the toys used in play. The toys developed for females are usually unidimensional (used for only one kind of play), not designed to encourage manipulation, exploration, or the examination of their mechanical parts. Girls usually receive a small number of large and unvaried toys. Boys usually have many small toys with many moving parts that provide opportunities for constructing, manipulating and reconstruction, and encourage creative problem solving and thinking. Games for girls and boys also differ. "Girls participate in highly structured, turn-taking games, regulated by invariable procedural rules that include fewer players and less often require contingency strategies. Boys' games, while rule-governed, reward initiative and improvisation, involve teams made up of peers, and encourage both within-team and between team (sic) competition" (Block, 1981, p. 44). Consider, for example, a game of softball as opposed to a game of jacks.

WHAT SHOULD WE DO
TO NURTURE GIFTEDNESS IN GIRLS?

Many of the characteristics and environmental conditions which seem to contribute to the lack of achievement by gifted girls are amenable to change. The sections which follow are intended to provide ideas for change. The whole realm of needed changes cannot be explored here; therefore, these ideas are given as suggested directions—a place to begin.

General Environmental Changes

One of the most fundamental changes that needs to be made is in our differential treatment of males and females. The literature clearly suggests that we must consistently make attempts to provide girls and boys the same opportunities to develop a sense of competence and capability through providing equal opportunity for exploration, equal opportunity to succeed at all kinds of tasks, equal instruction and rewards for achievement, equal encouragement to try new tasks, and equal attention regardless of sex. Changes in our adult behaviors will occur only if we first recognize our history of discriminatory, differential treatment. Try to monitor your behavior toward boys and girls to determine whether you exhibit any of the behaviors which might contribute to differential perceptions and success.

Selecting a School for a Young Gifted Child

Many parents of gifted children choose preschools using criteria which focus only on the academic or cognitive aspects of the program. Others are rightly concerned with the degree to which the social and emotional needs of their child will be effectively addressed. The parent of the young gifted girl must also be concerned with the degree to which the role models, the materials, and the activities of the preschool reflect nonsexist values. Are both males and females encouraged *and* rewarded for playing at the block center and the kitchen center? Are female professionals invited to share with the children? Do they see only female teachers and male administrators? Do the stories read to the children reflect both male and female characters in action and decision-making roles? Do the young girls have the same opportunity to answer questions? Are their answers given the same respect as those of the young boys? Are playground activities segregated by sex? All of these are questions which should be considered in selecting a preschool. They also are questions which should be raised when a gifted girl begins elementary school.

Play, Toys and Books

In addition to carefully avoiding stereotypic statements and other behaviors which indicate who "should" play with what toys, parents and teachers of both sexes can positively influence the development of young gifted children by becoming directly involved in small group play with toys and activities which represent traditional orientations to sex roles. For example, mothers should encourage children of both sexes, while actively participating, in the building of models; fathers can participate in the playing of house by "taking care of the baby" or "baking a cake;" mothers might play soccer and fathers might jump rope. In addition, it is important that girls not only be allowed, but that they be encouraged, to engage in the same play activities as boys. This guideline includes dressing girls in clothes that allow roughhousing rather than just observing and allowing them the same freedom to go across streets, to stay at a friend's house, to use scissors, etc., that is accorded to boys of the same age.

Teachers in preschools, kindergarten and the primary grades will often find that children have already developed stereotypic notions of who "should" play with what toys before they come to school and that they resist involvement with nonstereotpyic toys or games (O'Brien et al., 1983). One way to counter such attitudes is to integrate the play areas. For example, the "housekeeping" area may include a garage and some building or repair tools, and the block area may be made less stereotypic by the inclusion of doll furniture and small people normally reserved by the doll area.

The literature that is read to children has explicit messages about appropriate roles. Both parents and teachers should be very alert to the roles portrayed. For example, seemingly harmless nursery rhymes from Mother Goose often are extremely stereotypic. Consider Little Bo Peep who sits and waits for the sheep to come home in contrast to Little Jack Horner who declares, "What a good boy am I," even after destroying the pie! It is not necessary to ignore traditional children's books but it is necessary to talk about the roles, to present balanced pictures of the possible roles, and to point out blatant stereotyping.

As children begin to read on their own (which the gifted girl may begin to do very early) and to use textbooks in school, the books should be scrutinized for balance in the presentation of males and females in active roles, in occupations, in values, and attitudes. Identify books for the young gifted girl in which girls are given active roles, in which women are given professional roles, in which females are problem solvers and in control of their own environments, and in which solutions to problems are not trite or cliched. Look for biographies of gifted women and nonfiction books which present puzzles, suggest scientific investigations that can be done by the child, or encourage exploration and observation of the environment. (In a recent assessment of elementary age children, more boys than girls knew why a ball thrown in the air falls back to earth!). In addition, adults can intentionally become positive influences on the young gifted girl's learning by guiding her selection of books; by encouraging her to anticipate the possible consequences of certain actions, and to project solutions to mysteries before reading about or hearing the solution; by encouraging her to try to solve complex puzzles, to build models or design structures, to actually try simple science experiments and to explain the outcomes; and by encouraging her to actively explore her world through play.

A FINAL WORD

This article only begins to address all of the factors which seem to influence the development of the gifted girl, but clearly we are in a position to recognize the influence of environment on the differential achievement of males and females *and* we are in a position to do something about those environmental factors as parents, teachers, and other professionals. The question is not whether it is possible to change the effects of home, school, and community on gifted females, but whether we are willing to recognize our personal responsibilities and begin to alter *our* behavior for the benefit of gifted girls.

Preventing Severe Underachievement and Developing Achievement Motivation

Joanne Rand Whitmore, PhD

ABSTRACT. The success of the Cupertino Program for Under-achieving Gifted Students in the primary grades has informed us regarding the classroom conditions that may foster or prevent early school failure by our brightest and most creative youngsters. Analyses of the children's perceptions of their prior school experiences suggested controllable forces in classrooms that shape patterns of underachievement; without appropriate curricular programming, teacher guidance, and peer relationships, gifted children often learn to underachieve. Through applying our understanding of the motivational dynamics affecting the behavior of gifted children in school, we can design early educational programs that will motivate full participation and high academic achievement; that is, the principal rationale for providing appropriate gifted education in early childhood.

I was shocked at the school psychologist's report on David! There is no way I will recommend him for the gifted program even if he did somehow, miraculously, score 155 I.Q. on the Stanford-Binet! He is too immature and unmotivated! His work, when it gets done, and that is seldom, is messy and careless. He spends a lot of time daydreaming, and doesn't even make friends or get along with his classmates. If he is so bright, he certainly keeps it a secret in *my* classroom!

That's the way I felt when I was told Stephen qualified for the gifted program with a very high I.Q. score! Only he is different in that all of his energy goes into socializing—incessant

Joanne Rand Whitmore is Assistant Dean for Teacher Education and Professor of Early Childhood Education and Special Education at Kent State University. She is the author of the 1980 publication, *Giftedness, Conflict, and Underachievement* and is co-author with C. June Maker of the recent publication, *Intellectual Giftedness in Disabled Persons*. She has recently served in the presidency of The Association for the Gifted (TAG), a division of the Council for Exceptional Children (CEC).

talking, endless joking and storytelling, teasing others un-
mercifully, and just fooling around. He seems totally undisciplined and *never* completes his work on time! He always has a
million excuses, too! I think he is very creative, especially in
artwork and creating imaginative stores—and, in manipulating
me! But, he is not even performing on grade level in basic subjects, and certainly is not *that* motivated to work hard and
achieve!

It was through hearing comments such as these made by first and
second grade teachers in Cupertino, California, that I was led to the
discovery that significant numbers of primary-age gifted children
were being identified as low achievers with serious emotional and
social problems. These children were discovered to be intellectually
gifted by virtue of high performance on standardized measures of
intellectual ability, administered individually by school psychologists, as a consequence of a referral based on the results of a
required comprehensive assessment completed on every child. In
kindergarten, each child was evaluated on tests of readiness, aptitude, and achievement for use in educational planning. During first
grade, indications of special educational needs were explored further by more comprehensive testing and observations; where giftedness or disabilities were identified, appropriate placements and
special supplementary services were determined for implementation
no later than grade two.

To explore the extent to which a special class for underachieving
gifted students might be needed in our school system, all principals
in 27 elementary schools were invited to distribute descriptive information about the possible experimental intervention project and to
submit referrals to the coordinator of the district's gifted program.
Teachers and school psychologists were asked to identify any
students in the primary grades who had evidenced, in some way, exceptionally high intellectual ability but were doing poorly in schoolwork, scored low on achievement tests, and perhaps manifested
social and emotional "problems." The first year there were 57
referrals with 45 meeting all criteria for inclusion; the 22 children
evidencing the most critical need for special educational intervention were accepted for participation in a self-contained class for
underachieving gifted students. Details of that program and its
results, described elsewhere (Whitmore, 1980), served as the foundation of this article.

The Cupertino Project for Underachieving Gifted (UAG) Students, in the initial years of operation (1968-1970), was 100% successful in reversing patterns of early school failure and severe socioemotional maladjustment to create highly motivated and successful participants in the gifted program within a year or two. Although the group of children in the UAG Program contained diverse characteristics, there were many consistent descriptors in their records: "lazy, unmotivated"; "immature"; "messy and careless, undisciplined worker"; "has no real friends"; "has a very negative attitude toward school"; "evidences very low self-esteem." More than 95% of the referrals were males and all had been retained or considered for retention.

Descriptions of the behavioral problems of UAG children clustered into two patterns: (a) acute withdrawal with apparent immunity to teacher influence, or (b) highly disruptive, aggressive, attention-seeking behavior. In either case, the child was described as a social isolate who did not know how to relate effectively to other children—tending to be "bossy," argumentative, and demanding when interacting with peers or simply not relating to others. Low self-esteem was reflected in defensive reactions to criticism, mistakes, and teasing by peers. High anxiety was manifested in avoidance behavior, physical tension and high activity levels, unusual fears and phobias, refusal to engage in risk-taking, and nervous habits or tics. Many were described as having symptoms of serious psychological disorders and therapy had been recommended.

The successful intervention program validated the assumption upon which it was based: that gifted children are not born with the characteristics of "underachievers" but rather develop those attributes as their perceptions, attitudes, and behavior are shaped by specific elements and forces of the school experience. In other words, gifted children may learn to underachieve as they struggle to cope with discomfiting psychological conflict in the classroom. Parents of Cupertino UAG students had been perplexed by early school reports of their child's disinterest, poor work habits and performance, failure to follow directions and to participate with effort. In the preschool years, their child had evidenced a high drive to master knowledge and skills, persisted with high motivation to complete complex projects or to learn about advanced interests, and evidenced high ability to learn and to communicate with exceptional facility. The child initially had been enthusiastic about going to school, but the parents had seen the eagerness fade rather quickly and patterns of hesitation, procrastination, and avoidance emerge— finally expressed in very negative statements about school. Parents did not understand the cause of the change they had observed and conversations with teachers seemed to discuss two different children: one at home and one at school.

To understand the changes that occurred in these young highly gifted children, it is helpful to apply the knowledge we have gained from research about self-concepts, self-esteem, and behavior. Children do not come to school with a self-concept for school achievement. They possess specific self-concepts and consequent expectations for being able to learn and to solve problems, relate to peers and adults, and the like, but it is during the first three or four years of school that each child gradually formulates a stable self-concept that predicts future outcomes of effort in school, creates expectancies for relative success or failure socially and academically. Simultaneously, patterns of behavior are shaped by the extent to which the child perceives meaningful rewards or reinforcement accruing from efforts to conform and achieve. Therefore, the first years of school provide critical opportunities to prevent or reverse tendencies toward underachievement by shaping the individual child's perceptions and behaviors in positive ways to foster motivation to participate and achieve. Purkey's (1984) description of invitational teaching provides excellent guidance as to how to effectively nurture in students positive, realistic self-concepts for school achievement; healthy levels of self-esteem; and belief in personal ability to participate successfully.

By understanding the specific motivational dynamics of gifted young children and the forces shaping classroom behavior, parents and teachers can prevent or reverse patterns of academic underachievement (Whitmore, 1978, 1979, 1980). Intervention is most effective in the first three years of school when the perceptions, self-concept, and behavior patterns are being formed. The remainder of this article will provide some basic information to guide those efforts.

FORCES SHAPING THE DEVELOPMENT OF PATTERNS OF ACADEMIC UNDERACHIEVEMENT

The field of early childhood education has been built upon a base of research that has established those years as critical to the development of self-perceptions and self-esteem, social competence, emotional adjustment, specific cognitive abilities and personal values. It is those characteristics of children that interact with the school environment and experiences to shape patterns of behavior reflecting relatively high or low motivation to achieve academically. Through intensive study of individual children in the Cupertino UAG Project, the acute vulnerability of young gifted children (particularly those more highly gifted and creative) to motivational difficulties and patterns of underachievement became very clear. It is very important to recognize that the special characteristics and needs that seemingly made the Cupertino UAG children so vulnerable were identified also by outstanding, high-achieving adolescents (American Association for Gifted Children, 1978). That vulnerability must be understood as a basis for designing school experiences that will prevent or reverse underachievement in young gifted children.

Special Socialization Needs

The highly gifted children in Cupertino, who developed severe behavior problems and failed academically in the first years of school, evidenced specific socialization needs that made them vulnerable to psychosocial conflict in school. First of all, they were functioning at very immature levels of social competence, lacking understanding of themselves and others. This developmental deficit seemingly was caused by very limited experience with agemates and group activities. Advanced mental abilities often led to the development of advanced interests, causing a lack of commonality with agemates; thus, patterns of play in isolation or tagging along after older children had developed. Few of the children had participated in even a part-time preschool program. Consequently, upon arrival at school the child had difficulty sharing, participating in a group activity, waiting for a turn, and accepting not being "center-stage" or in control of the whole activity.

A second area of social vulnerability was the emotional conflict created by tension between the required conformity in school and the child's intense desire to express individuality. Tendencies to behave independently more than to cooperate, to think divergently and critically, often had resulted in peer teasing, teacher admonishment, and other social penalties which are difficult for a gifted child to accept. The child who was inclined to withdraw from conflict had begun to function more in isolation, often escaping into fantasy. The child with a more aggressive response to conflict had tended to become the class "clown" or "bully." In either case, feelings of alienation and isolation had been created.

The gifted child is vulnerable to social discomfort and difficulty in the classroom because of several specific requirements of that social setting. Teachers expect children to dependably follow directions, not give them; to participate cooperatively in group activities, not function independently in isolated activity; and to exhibit reasonable levels of self-control, not impulsive behavior. Furthermore, despite academic rhetoric about classroom climates that affirm diversity in our society, there still is a powerful press on highly creative and gifted children to not be so different, to adapt to the social setting, to blend in. All of these factors make the gifted child very vulnerable to social conflict in school.

Personality Attributes and Emotional Conflict

In addition to a potential lack of social competence and comfort, young gifted children tend to possess some personality characteristics that make them vulnerable to emotional conflict, as described earlier by Roedell. Three attributes of highly gifted and creative children in the UAG Program were major causes of the severe emotional disturbance reported by parents and teachers.

The first source of intense psychological conflict is the potential interaction between the child's trait of perfectionism and the perception of failure to meet expectations of self, teachers, and parents. In essence, this conflict is generated by the severe gap between the youngster's level of intellectual ability or mental age and the actual performance level on intellectual or academic tasks in school. The child is inclined to make invidious comparisons of self with agemates and intellectual peers, a natural occurrence which is especially problematic for those young gifted children who have developmental delays or low ability in developmental areas that affect school performance (e.g., motor skills, perception, and eye-hand coordination).

A second area of emotional vulnerability very prevalent among gifted underachievers is an interaction between the personal trait of supersensitivity and the perceived messages from teachers, parents, and peers providing evaluative feedback. There is a definite tendency on the part of many gifted children to interpret criticism and mistakes as rejection and failure. Laughter or humorous comments in response to an error or an expressed idea tends to be interpreted as ridicule. Thus, the child develops a tendency to avoid a public display of his/her abilities that may elicit such negative messages.

The third area of conflict is that which may be generated between the child's natural characteristics of intrinsic motivation and independence and the emphasis in school on extrinsic rewards. After years at home of independent pursuit of the child's interests which was very satisfying and intrinsically rewarding, the school's emphasis on grades, awards in competition, or punishment for noncompliance often fails to motivate these highly gifted children. Instructions to do something "because I said so" does not persuade such a highly gifted, creative child to conform. Pressure tactics and threats are most ineffective, often eliciting passive resistance or outright rebellion.

Factors Shaping the Development of Low Motivation and Underachievement

Gifted children are particularly vulnerable to low motivation and achievement in school when there is a substantive difference between the youngster's learning style and/or academic needs and the curriculum and instruction provided in the kindergarten-primary grades. The more highly gifted and creative the child, the greater the psychological conflict and the vulnerability to underachievement and lack of motivation to participate.

Young gifted children who have developed high initiative in pursuing special interests and satisfying their curiosity come to school with a sense of independence and ability to manage, to some extent, their own learning. The more independent, autonomous learner dislikes the emphasis of early education on following directions and tends to be bored by the predictable routines. Typically, the child who becomes unmotivated to complete work complains of excessive repetition of what he/she already knows and has mastered, but also seems to find little personal satisfaction in convergent thinking exercises and longs for more opportunity for creative self-expression, scientific problem solving, play with words and ideas, and exciting exploration of the world. Frequently, parents of these children have rewarded creative behavior at home, reinforced independence and self-directed learning, and responded to their intense pursuit of self-expression or discovery. Consequently, the severely limited opportunities for kindergarten and primary-age children to enjoy that learning style in school may result in a steady decline in desire to participate in school.

A major factor contributing to the development of low motivation and academic achievement for gifted children is the rigidity of educational planning for young children. In their efforts to guarantee that every young child becomes equipped for success through mastery of basic skills in the early grades, teachers regrettably have been forced by district policies, parent pressures, or personal beliefs to adhere rigidly to a predetermined sequence of skill development activities. This practice, nearly a matter of public policy across this country now, places accelerated, more mature gifted students in great jeopardy motivationally as well as the gifted students who may be relatively immature and lacking in readiness for reading and writing tasks.

Youngsters entering with advanced knowledge and skills tend to be unrewarded by task completion, learning quickly to pace themselves to avoid another sheet of the same activity! The curriculum content, as well as traditional mode of instruction, do not produce the feelings of satisfaction gained in independent out-of-school activities or learning at home. The lack of challenge and sense of accomplishment decrease motivation to do the work. In contrast, the gifted child who lacks readiness for reading and/or writing because of mild developmental delays, specific learning disabilities, or a lack of needed prior experience, may begin to avoid academic tasks because of the intense frustration they engender, the feelings of "dumbness" and inadequacy they create, and the sense of failure they produce. In either case, the young child with exceptional potential for high academic achievement may become motivated to avoid the schoolwork, to escape into daydreams or independent projects, and to avoid participation that in any way elevates the expectations of the teachers and parents.

To summarize, the social experiences of the young gifted child in school, the emotional conflict generated by personal desires and expectations, and the nature of the curriculum and instruction of the kindergarten-primary grades can contribute to the development of low motivation to participate and to achieve in school. The "problem" of underachievement must be viewed not as the child's laziness or lack of motivation but rather as the product of his/her interaction with the social and intellectual environment and learning opportunities experienced in school. To prevent or reverse a tendency toward low effort and achievement in the early grades, parents and teachers must work together (a) to help the child learn to understand and cope constructively with the school experience, and to become more self-disciplined; and (b) to design an appropriate educational program that will stimulate motivation to achieve by inviting the child to participate successfully in meaningful learning activities.

PREVENTING OR REVERSING EARLY PATTERNS OF UNDERACHIEVEMENT

Parents can do much to guide their gifted child's development of self-understanding, a realistic and positive self-concept, healthy self-esteem, effective coping strategies, social competence, self-discipline and self-management, and intellectual giftedness. When motivation, however, to attend and participate in school is declining and significant underachievement is occurring, the parents must advocate for the child's needs and insist upon a skillful evaluation of the school experience in relation to the youngster's characteristics and needs. The gifted population is diverse and specific factors contributing to the development of negative attitudes and underachievement vary among individuals, but critical elements have been identified to guide an evaluation of alternatives available to gifted children in a community—teachers, classrooms and schools (Whitmore, 1983, 1984). The conditions that tend to prevent or reverse early patterns of underachievement will be discussed briefly in relation to the critical factors of the teacher, peers, and the curriculum. More detailed descriptions can be found in Whitmore (1978, 1979, 1980, 1985).

Characteristics of the Effective Teacher

It is obvious that the most critical factor to be considered in attempting to prevent or reverse patterns of underachievement is the selection of the best teacher for the child. Although district policies may restrict what the teacher can do to modify curriculum and instruction for the child, effective teachers generally finds ways to accommodate each child's needs reasonably well and create a social and emotional climate that fosters motivated participation.

Effective teachers of gifted students have an accurate understanding of the nature of giftedness (particularly, what it is and is not) and the special needs of young gifted children. They recognize the unevenness of development across areas; the potential lack of readiness for some standard activities (e.g., writing, reading); and the vulnerability of young gifted children to fears of failure, destructive self-criticism, and social discomfort. Effective teachers carefully assess the child's readiness for specific learning activities and seek to make participation rewarding; they may remove segments of the curriculum associated with repeated failure to destroy the phobia and rebuild positive attitudes toward it through later activities designed to create success and enjoyment.

Strategies of motivating participation are the focus of planning, and pressure tactics and punishment for nonparticipation or failure to meet expectations are avoided. The teachers view mistakes as a natural part of learning when a student is adequately challenged, and evaluate student achievement based on test performance when mastery has been achieved rather than on daily practice work. Overall, these teachers enjoy gifted children, respect their special abilities, trust them to be dependable with responsibilities; and they establish a warm, authentic relationship of open, sensitive communication with students. The accepting and understanding relationships between these teachers and young gifted students nurture positive feelings about being in the classroom, participating in activities, and expending effort to achieve.

Gifted children should be placed with teachers who are skilled in providing guidance in the classroom to individuals and groups in order to foster (a) the development of self-understanding relative to strengths and weaknesses in abilities; (b) constructive skills for coping with feelings of frustration, boredom, anger, alienation; and (c) skills of self-discipline and the self-management of learning. These teachers capitalize on the natural abilities of gifted children (especially characteristics of high independence, initiative, problem solving and evaluation skills) to encourage the rapid development of self-directed learning in the classroom. They not only stimulate continually the higher intellectual abilities of the children but model appropriate values of creative thinking, problem solving, productivity, and independence. In addition to all of the above characteristics, effective teachers of young gifted students are distinguished by their consistent modification of curriculum and instruction to meet the specific needs of individual children.

The Important Role of Peers

Gifted children need to be placed in classrooms where there are at least three to five intellectual peers and the potential of developing at least one very good friend, a "buddy." All children need a sense of belonging and having a friend, but gifted children are especially vulnerable to feelings of isolation, alienation, and rejection because of the nature of their differentness. At least a small group of peers is essential to avoid having the gifted child often working alone, doing things differently from the rest of the class, and being able to dominate intellectually. Through stimulating debates, discussions, and cooperative work projects with intellectual peers the gifted student will be more challenged and, thus, more satisfied in the learning process. To have the companionship of other students who share similar interests, abilities, projects, and goals reduces the sense of aloneness and facilitates the development of social competence through opportunities to interact while learning.

Gifted students benefit greatly from frequent opportunities to engage in social problem solving in which they receive feedback from others that informs them as to how others perceive and react to them. By receiving honest feedback from classmates regarding responses to their behavior, gifted students can be guided to consider the consequences of their choices in social interaction, to understand group dynamics, and to understand that they can control social reaction to them by listening carefully to feedback and altering their patterns of behavior. The development of social understanding and skills will be facilitated by the presence of at least a few intellectual peers and the probability of developing self-enhancing friendships will be increased, both of which are essential to high motivation to participate and achieve in school.

Characteristics of an Effective Curriculum

Gifted children are naturally motivated to master knowledge and skills and to satisfy their curiosity in areas of interest to them. That is how we most often recognize giftedness in young children. In a classroom in which the teacher provides learning experiences that are intrinsically rewarding as well as externally reinforced, are perceived by students to be meaningful and valuable, allow frequent opportunities to pursue and expand personal interests, stimulate awareness of potential careers, and utilize a variety of methods and materials, gifted students overall show high motivation to participate and achieve. There are four specific characteristics of an effective curriculum that deserve some elaboration.

As has been mentioned earlier, effective programs for young gifted students are designed to accommodate the assessed strengths and weaknesses of each individual child. The majority of time each day is spent in rewarding development of the child's strengths with appropriate remediation of developmental weaknesses occurring efficiently. Motivating interests are incorporated into the remedial curriculum and the process of learning involves student problem solving, evaluative thinking, and creativity wherever possible. Intensive, short periods of effectively designed instruction for remediation of deficit skills or weaknesses permit higher levels of concentration and reduce the amount of frustration. Such an approach proved highly successful in Cupertino where students averaged 3 years of gain on standardized tests of reading ability at the end of 9 months of participation in the UAG class (Whitmore, 1980).

The second critical attribute of an effective curriculum is the provision of ample opportunity throughout the day to engage in inquiry, higher level thinking, problem solving, creativity, and self-expression. This requires both a balance between skill development activities and the arts and sciences curricula, and the systematic use and development of the gifted child's special abilities and needs throughout *all* instruction. Active involvement in wondering, hypothesizing, experimenting, exploring, probing, discovering, and the like is usually highly motivating to underachievers, most of whom are boys in the early grades who find sitting still to engage in passive, routine practice to be very difficult.

The third essential element of an effective curriculum to motivate academic achievement in young gifted children is the systematic provision of affective education. The selection of literature and reading materials, topics for units of study in the sciences and arts, and activities to facilitate learning in basic curricular areas can contribute to the development of self-understanding, understanding and acceptance of others, healthier levels of self-esteem and sense of efficacy, more realistic self-concepts and expectations, and greater social competence. The selection of reading materials and topics of study can address objectives related to the children's need to understand human nature, the nature of specific abilities and disabilities, the causes of behavior, and the like. Class meetings to plan, evaluate, or problem solve can be an important part of affective education as well as individual guidance sessions, group discussions of literature, and self-expression through the arts (e.g., role playing, drama, poetry, painting). All of these activities, along with increased student responsibility for learning, convey respect, trust, and belief in the child's ability. Thus, an outcome of such educational planning tends to be enhanced self-perceptions as well as increased social competence.

The fourth element of an effective curriculum is the development in children of constructive coping strategies and self-modification techniques, building upon their increasing self-understanding. This involves helping students identify the cause of the behavior that interferes with participation and achievement, to recognize its emergence just prior to its disruption of achievement-oriented behavior, and to find an alternative way to meet the physiological or psychological need to avoid disrupting others and to allow quick return to the task. For example, a child recognizing an impulse to move or hit someone might elect to run the track, hit a tether ball, or squeeze clay at the art center for a few minutes. A child having difficulty concentrating might learn to remove him/herself from the group temporarily by working in an isolated "office" (special partitioned table) or sitting in another location. Muscle tension often contributes to distractibility so simple exercises of the neck, shoulders, arms and legs can restore a more relaxed feeling and an ability to concentrate. Similarly, alternative ways of handling such problems as tendencies to be "bossy," to explode with temper, or to have difficulty controlling talking can be found by the child through guided problem solving.

In sum, the curriculum must be redesigned to more closely fit the special needs of the child in social, emotional, and academic curricular areas. An understanding and skilled teacher and a few intellectual peers are the most important factors. There is substantial evidence that, under the conditions described above, underachievement and low motivation to participate in school can be drastically reduced or eliminated in most young gifted children.

CONCLUDING COMMENTS
ABOUT THE POTENTIAL EFFECTS
OF EARLY EDUCATION

The Cupertino UAG Project demonstrated that, in fact, school experience can be hazardous to the mental health and achievement motivation of young gifted children. Rather than facilitating the development of exceptional potential for learning and academic achievement, it can produce damaging effects on the child's perceptions of self and others, attitudes toward school, and social competence. The result can be the transformation over a period of 1-3 years from a highly motivated and confident learner, eager to go to school, to a child described as unmotivated, lazy, and a social isolate, with signs of very low self-esteem. In relatively short time, the child may have learned that efforts are unrewarded in school, participation brings social penalties and discomfort, and it is safer, more comfortable not to try and to fail than to try to meet expectations and then fail. Underachievement can be learned!

Yet, in the Cupertino Project, all primary-age children were successfully re-educated to discover their potential for success and personal satisfaction in school, to know how to make friends and function competently in group activities, to hold more realistic expectations for themselves derived from more accurate understandings of self and human nature, and to gain control over outcomes of their efforts in school by the development of self-discipline and skills for self-managed learning. The result was the return of 80% of the first class to self-contained classes for high-achieving gifted students after one year of intervention; six students required one or two more years before returning to gifted or regular classrooms.

Follow-up evaluations (reported in Whitmore, 1980) showed sustained effects relative to the maintenance of more positive, realistic self-concepts for school achievement, higher levels of self-esteem and sense of efficacy, and more constructive coping mechanisms. Most of the UAG students became high academic achievers, several distinguishing themselves with very high honors in high school and college. Some produced good but less remarkable academic records, but developed their giftedness while coping effectively with schools and society. In other words, the most important outcomes of restored mental health and effective coping and social skills were achieved with all, as well as satisfying development of their chosen special talent or giftedness. Most of them produced outstanding academic records, also.

The findings of the Cupertino UAG Project provide a rationale for the importance of early identification and programming for gifted children. Less severely underachieving children and even exceptionally high achievers (AAGC, 1978) evidence the same vulnerabilities as were found to have been contributing factors shaping the development of patterns of underachievement and low motivation to participate in school. In essence, the message is that if identification and programming do not occur until after the early grades, many gifted children may have developed negative perceptions, low motivation, and patterns of underachievement that may impair their academic performance or limit their educational opportunities throughout the elementary and secondary years.

To provide educational conditions that prevent underachievement is not costly or particularly difficult to deliver; it simply requires trained teachers, clustering gifted peers in regular or special classrooms, and providing the motivating, invitational climate and an appropriately modified curriculum. It is more costly for society to lose the potential intellectual and social contributions of these gifted individuals in the future, and it is much more difficult to reverse patterns of underachievement in later years after attitudes and behavior patterns have been established. The prevention of underachievement and lost potential is the rationale for comprehensive assessment upon entry to school and appropriate modifications in the educational program from the beginning days of school.

Summary and Conclusions

Since giftedness has been redefined as potential for the exceptional development of specific abilities and thus for high achievement in areas related to those special abilities, the importance of providing appropriate early educational experiences to nurture the development of such potential is obvious. Recent brain research lends new, objective support to the longstanding belief that the child's environment (particularly the people in it—i.e., parents, teachers, and peers) critically influences the extent to which optimal intellectual abilities and giftedness develop. Furthermore, additional evidence has accumulated to establish the fact that special attributes of young gifted children make them vulnerable to social and emotional difficulties and to significant intellectual/academic underachievement. The vulnerability of young gifted children creates special educational needs, which provide the structure of a defensible rationale for programs designed to meet these particular needs in order to prevent socioemotional difficulties and underachievement. The gifted population is at "high risk" educationally, as are the handicapped, and share the same civil rights to early intervention and appropriate programming that was guaranteed to disabled children under Public Law 94-142. Gifted children need similar protection of these basic educational rights.

Gifted children are at high risk developmentally and motivationally if their special characteristics are not recognized and their educational needs are not accommodated by appropriate programming, just like develpmentally delayed or disabled youngsters. Psychological conflict between their personal needs and the demands and opportunities of the environment make them vulnerable to emotional stress and frustration, social discomfort if not feelings of alienation, and a lack of motivation to participate in educational opportunities to fully develop their exceptional potential for intellectual achievement. Young boys seem particularly vulnerable to disruptive behavior problems and severe degrees of academic underachievement in school because of their active, investigative learning styles and a tendency to be less ready for traditional academic tasks requiring reading and writing. Females are vulnerable in the early years because the seeds of underachievement may be sown as girls are not encouraged to fully develop all intellectual abilities, and are not provided models and incentives to foster high achievement motivation beyond conforming and earning "good grades."

Appropriate education in the early years provides an intervention to prevent the underdevelopment of exceptional potential and to foster the high achievement of gifted individuals. Such early intervention is perhaps most critical for gifted youngsters in economically disadvantaged, culturally different/minority populations, and handicapped populations where adequate stimulation of higher intellectual abilities and educational aspirations are less apt to be nurtured. It is clear, however, that appropriate early education is critical to the prevention of significant underachievement in many, if not all, intellectually gifted children for motivational reasons: to prevent males from becoming early school failures and "behavior problems," and to prevent females from later underachievement created by high conformity needs and a lack of awareness of one's intellectual and career potential.

An appropriate education for gifted children provides an integrative approach, as described by Barbara Clark (1983, 1986), to optimally stimulate the development of all brain functions. Through appropriate stimulation, the full development of all cognitive abilities is achieved. Additionally, young gifted children need well-planned affective education that helps them acquire self-understanding, social competence, and sound mental health. An appropriate educational program always allows for uneven development, nurturing the child's strengths while strengthening the areas of relative weakness. It involves flexibility grouping children together for appropriately challenging activities that provide content enrichment while accelerating the pace of learning according to the readiness of individual students.

The obstacles to providing appropriate early childhood education programs for gifted and talented children arise from both real and artificial issues. The issue of whether or not they can be identified in the early years is an artificial one, except perhaps for populations for which perceptions tend to be negatively biased against the possibility of giftedness. Precise behavioral observations and reports of parents and teachers, along with interviews of children, can provide reliable evidence of intellectual giftedness. Whether or not young gifted children should be identified is a real issue. The effects of labelling a child depends on society's treatment of a child so labelled and the meaning attributed to the label. In homes or communities where there are inappropriate adult expectations held for gifted students, based on misunderstandings and a lack of accurate information about the nature of giftedness, identification can be a negative liability for the child. In other circumstances, it can be a positive benefit to the child in every way.

The questionable value of early intervention is a false issue. It has been well established that early intervention can prevent underachievement and school failure, severe social and emotional maladjustment, and the extremely negative effects of deprivation in economically disadvantaged homes. It also stands to reason that early detection of exceptional cognitive abilities could have a very positive effect on the design of educational intervention programs with handicapped children. And, no one will seriously challenge the value of early intervention and prevention for high-risk populations, of which gifted children are a part. Positive early education is desirable for *all* children.

The fact that there are too few teachers in regular educational programs who understand the special needs of gifted children and are skilled in nurturing the full development of their special abilities is a real issue. The fact that many school systems have established policies that mitigate against appropriate educational provisions for gifted children, and that teacher training programs also generally have neglected that area of professional competence, are two important issues. If all teachers were trained and required to provide adequately for individual needs, and were accurately informed about the needs of gifted students, then gifted education would be a very different field.

Another real issue is the lack of assistance and support provided parents. It is very difficult yet for parents to acquire accurate information about the characteristics and needs of gifted children. They generally begin to feel desperate in their desire to become skilled in how to handle the child's need for discipline and ways of coping with frustration; the child's demand for answers to very complex questions and a defensible rationale for everything; and the child's intense drive to understand phenomena. Parents need a network of emotional support and advocacy for the needs of gifted children and their families. They need access to helpful agencies as resources for guidance and information regarding educational alternatives.

The substance of the issues or obstacles discussed does not legitimatize resistance to the establishment of appropriate educational programs for young gifted children. The young gifted child population still is the most neglected and, thus, educationally retarded (Marland, 1972). Beginning programming for gifted and talented students at grade four obviously is too late; prevention is far easier and more successful than later remedial or corrective intervention. Early childhood educators must be prepared to better meet the needs of young gifted children, with the support of understanding administrators. Teachers must continue to tap into and nurture the potentialities within every young child; therefore, we must continually seek to appropriately stimulate, challenge, and guide the development of gifted children in the early years.

Bibliography

Abroms, K. I. (1983). Affective development. In M. B. Karnes (Ed.), *The underserved: Our young gifted children* (pp. 118-143). Reston, VA: Council for Exceptional Children.

Achenbach, T. M. (1970). Standardization of a research instrument for identifying associative responding in children. *Developmental Psychology, 2*, 283-291.

Albert, R. (1978). Observations and suggestions regarding giftedness, familial influence and the achievement of eminence. *The Gifted Child Quarterly, 22*, 201-211.

Alexander, P. J., & Skinner, M. E. (1980). The effects of early entrance on subsequent social and academic development: A followup study. *Journal for the Education of the Gifted, 3*(3), 147-150.

Alvino, J. (Ed.). (1985). *Parents' guide to raising a gifted child: Recognizing and developing your child's potential.* Boston: Little, Brown & Co.

American Association for Gifted Children (1978). *On being gifted.* New York: Walker & Co.

Anastasi, A. (1976). *Psychological testing* (4th ed.). New York: Macmillan.

Bagnato, S. J., & Neisworth, J. T. (1979). Between assessment and intervention: Forging an assessment/curriculum linkage for the handicapped preschooler. *Child Care Quarterly, 8*, 179-195.

Bagnato, S. J., & Neisworth, J. T. (1980). The intervention efficiency index (IEI): An approach to preschool program accountability. *Exceptional Children, 46*, 264-269.

Bailey, D. B., & Leonard, J. (1977). A model for adapting Bloom's taxonomy to a preschool curriculum for the gifted. *Gifted Child Quarterly, 21*(1), 97-102.

Barbe, W. (1956). A study of the family background of the gifted. *Journal of Educational Psychology, 47*, 302-309.

Barbe, W. (1964). *One in a thousand: A comparative study of moderately and highly gifted elementary school children.* Columbus: Ohio State Department of Education.

Baum, S. (1984). Meeting the needs of learning disabled gifted students. *Roeper Review, 7*(1), 16-19.

Beckwith, C. (1971). Relationships between attributes of mothers and their infants' I.Q. scores. *Child Development, 42,* 1083-1097.

Benbow, C. P., & Stanley, J. C. (1980). Sex differences in mathematical ability. Fact or artifact? *Science, 210,* 1262-1264.

Birns, B. (1976). The emergence and socialization of sex role differences in the earliest years. *Merrill-Palmer Quarterly, 22,* 229-254.

Birns, B., & Golden, M. (1972). Prediction of intellectual performance at three years from infant test and personality measures. *Merrill-Palmer Quarterly, 18,* 53-58.

Block, J. H. (1981). The difference between boys and girls: How gender roles are shaped. *Principal, 60,* 41-45.

Bloom, B. (1982). The role of gifts and markers in the development of talents. *Exceptional Children, 48,* 510-521.

Bloom, B. S. (Ed.). (1985). *Developing talent in young people.* New York: Ballantine.

Bogen, J. E. (1977). Some educational aspects of hemispheric specialization. In M. C. Wittrock (Ed.), *The human brain* (pp. 133-152). Englewood Cliffs, NJ: Prentice-Hall.

Borland, J. (1979). Teacher identification of the gifted: A new look. *Journal for the Education of the Gifted, 2,* 20-33.

Borland, J. H. (in press). What happens to them all? A response to "What happens to the gifted girl?" In C. J. Maker (Ed.), *Defensible programs for the gifted.* Rockville, MD: Aspen.

Bower, R., Broughton, F., & Moore, M. (1970). Assessment of intention in sensorimotor infants. *Nature, 228,* 679-681.

Bradway, K. (1964). Jung's psychological types. *Journal of Analytical Psychology, 9,* 129-135.

Braga, J. L. (1971). Early admission: Opinion vs. evidence. *The Elementary School Journal, 72*(1), 35-46.

Brazelton, T. B., & Als, H. (1979). Four early stages in the development of mother-infant interaction. *Psychoanalytical Study of the Child, 34,* 349-369.

Buell, S., & Coleman, P. (1981). Quantitative evidence for selective dendritic growth in normal human aging but not in senile dementia. *Brain Research, 214*(1), 23-41.

Buros, O. K. (Ed.). (1972). *The seventh mental measurements year-book*. Highland Park, NJ: Gryphon Press.

Buzan, T. (1983). *Use both sides of your brain*. New York: E. P. Dutton.

Callahan, C. M. (1979). The gifted and talented woman. In A. H. Passow (Ed.), *The gifted and the talented: Their education and development*. The seventy-eighth yearbook of the National Society for the Study of Education, Part I (pp. 401-423). Chicago: University of Chicago Press.

Caplan, P. J., MacPherson, G. M., & Tobin, P. (1985). Do sex-related differences in spatial abilities really exist? A multilevel critique with new data. *American Psychologist, 40*, 786-799.

Cassidy, J., & Vukelich, C. (1980). Do the gifted read early? *The Reading Teacher, 33*(5), 578-582.

Chance, P. R. (1985). *The imposter phenomenon*. Atlanta, GA: Peachtree.

Cheyney, A. B. (1962). Parents view their intellectually gifted children. *Peabody Journal of Education, 40*, 98-101.

Ciha, T. E., Harris, T. E., Hoffman, C., & Potter, M. W. (1974). Parents as identifiers of giftedness, ignored but accurate. *The Gifted Child Quarterly, 18*, 191-195.

Clark, B. (1986). *Optimizing learning: The integrative education model in the classroom*. Columbus, OH: Charles E. Merrill.

Clark, B. (1983). *Growing up gifted* (2nd ed.). Columbus, OH: Charles E. Merrill.

Clarke-Stewart, K. (1973). Interactions between mothers and their young children: Characteristics and consequences. *Monographs of Society for Research in Child Development, 38*(153).

Coleman, J. (1961). *The adolescent society*. New York: Free Press.

Coleman, J. M., & Fults, B. A. (1982). Self-concept and the gifted classroom: The role of social comparison. *Gifted Child Quarterly, 26*(3), 116-120.

Coleman, J. M., & Fults, B. A. (1985). Special-class placement, level of intelligence, and the self-concepts of gifted children: A social comparison perspective. *RASE, 6*(1), 7-12.

Collins, W. A., Sobol, B. I., & Westby, S. (1981). Effects of adult commentary on children's comprehension and inferences about a televised aggressive portrayal. *Child Development, 52*, 158-163.

Conner, J. M., Schackman, M., & Serbin, L. A. (1978). Sex related differences in response to a visual-spatial test and generalized to a related test. *Child Development, 49*, 24-29.

Consortium for Longitudinal Studies. (1983). *As the twig is bent:*

Lasting effects of preschool programs. Hillsdale, NJ: Lawrence Erlbaum Associates, Publishers.

Cooley, D., Chauvin, J. C., & Karnes, F. A. (1984). Gifted females: A comparison of attitudes by male and female teachers. *Roeper Review, 6,* 164-165.

Cornell, D. G. (1983). Gifted children: The impact of positive labeling on the family system. *American Journal of Orthopsychiatry, 53,* 322-336.

Cox, R. L. (1977). Background characteristics of 456 gifted children. *The Gifted Child Quarterly, 21,* 261-267.

Crandall, V. J., Katkovsky, W., & Preston, A. (1962). Motivational and ability determinants of young children's intellectual achievement behaviors. *Child Development, 33,* 643-661.

Davis, J. A. (1964). *Great aspirations: The school plans of America's college seniors.* Chicago: Aldine.

Deaux, K. (1984). From individual differences to social categories: Analysis of a decade's research on gender. *American Psychologist, 39,* 105-116.

Deaux, K., & Farris, E. (1977). Attributing causes for one's own performance: The effects of sex, norms, and outcome. *Journal of Research in Personality, 11,* 59-72.

Diamond, M. (1980, May). Education and the brain. Lecture presented at the conference *The human brain: New frontiers in learning,* Los Angeles, CA.

Dunn, R. S., & Price, G. E. (1980). The learning style characteristics of gifted students. *Gifted Child Quarterly, 24*(1), 37-40.

Ehrlich, V. Z. (1978). *The Astor Program for gifted children: Prekindergarten through grade three.* Teachers College, Columbia University. Gifted Child Studies, 490 Hudson Street, New York, NY 10014.

Ehrlich, V. Z. (1978). *Program planning for the gifted.* Gifted Child Studies, 490 Hudson Street, New York, NY 10014.

Ehrlich, V. Z. (1980). Identifying giftedness in the early years, from three through seven. In S. Butterfield (Ed.), *Education of the preschool/primary gifted and talented.* National/State Leadership Training Institute, Ventura County Superintendent of Schools, 535 East Main Street, Ventura, CA 93009.

Ehrlich, V. Z. (1981). *Analysis of traits cited by parents in identifying young gifted children.* Presentation at the World Conference on the Gifted, Montreal, Canada.

Elardo, P., & Cooper, M. (1977). *AWARE*. Menlo Park, CA: Addison-Wesley.

Fagot, B. I. (1973). Sex related stereotyping of toddlers' behavior. *Developmental Psychology*, *9*, 429.

Fantz, R. (1961). The origin of form perception. *Scientific American*, *204*, 66-72.

Fox, L. H. (1977). *Changing behaviors and attitudes of gifted girls*. Paper presented at the annual meeting of the American Psychological Association, Washington, D.C.

Frisch, H. L. (1977). Sex stereotypes in adult-infant play. *Child Development*, *48*, 563-568.

Galbraith, J. (1985). The eight grade gripes of gifted kids: Responding to special needs. *Roeper Review*, *8*(1), 15-18.

Gallagher, J. J. (1979). Issues in education for the gifted. In A. H. Passow (Ed.), *The gifted and the talented: Their education and development*. The seventy-eighth yearbook of the National Society for the Study of Education, Part I (pp. 28-44). Chicago: University of Chicago Press.

Gallagher, J. J. (1985). Peer acceptance of highly gifted children in elementary school. *Elementary School Journal*, *58*, 465-470.

Galyean, B. (1977-80). *The confluent teaching of foreign languages* (ESEA Title IV-C Project, Year-end Reports). Los Angeles: Los Angeles City Unified Schools.

Galyean, B. (1978-81). *A confluent language program for K-3, NES LES students* (ESEA Title IV-C Project, Year-end Reports). Los Angeles: Los Angeles Unified Schools.

Garai, J. E., & Scheinfeld, A. (1968). Sex differences in mental and behavioral traits. *Genetic Psychology Monographs*, *77*, 169-299.

Gardner, H. (1983). *Frames of mind: The theory of multiple intelligences*. New York: Basic Books.

Gardner, J. (1971). *The development of object identity in the first six months of infancy*. Paper presented at the Biennial Meeting of the Society for Research in Child Development, Minneapolis, MN.

Gazzaniga, M., & LeDoux, J. (1978). *The integrated mind*. New York: Plenum Press.

Gear, G. (1978). Effects of training on teacher-judged giftedness. *The Gifted Child Quarterly*, *22*, 90-97.

Getzels, J. W., & Dillon, J. T. (1973). The nature of giftedness and the education of the gifted. In R.M.W. Travers (Ed.), *Second handbook of research on teaching* (pp. 689-731). Chicago: Rand McNally.

Gilligan, C. (1982). *In a different voice: Psychological theory and women's development.* Cambridge, MA: Harvard University Press.

Goddard, H. H. (1928). *School training of gifted children.* Yonkers-on-Hudson, NY: World Books.

Goertzel, M. G., Goertzel, V., & Goertzel, T. G. (1978). *Three hundred eminent personalities.* San Francisco: Jossey-Bass.

Goertzel, V., & Goertzel, M. G. (1962). *Cradles of eminence.* Boston: Little, Brown & Co.

Goldberg, S., & Lewis, M. (1969). Play behavior in the year-old infant: Early sex differences. *Child Development, 40,* 21-31.

Goldstein, A. G., & Chance, J. E. (1965). Effects of practice on sex-related differences in performance on embedded figures. *Psychonomic Science, 3,* 361-362.

Goodman, D. (1978). Learning from lobotomy. *Human Behavior,* (1), 44-49.

Guilford, J. (1967). *The nature of human intelligence.* New York: McGraw Hill.

Hagen, E. (1980). *Identification of the gifted.* New York: Teachers College Press.

Hanninen, G. E. (1984). Effectiveness of a preschool program for the gifted and talented. *Journal for the Education of the Gifted, 7*(3), 192-204.

Harris, D. B. (1963). *Children's drawing as measures of intellectual maturity.* New York: Harcourt Brace Jovanovich.

Hart, L. (1981). Brain, language, and new concepts of learning. *Educational Leadership, 39,* 443- 445.

Hart, L. (1983). *Human brain and human learning.* New York: Longman.

Harvey, J. C., & Katz, C. (1985). *If I'm so successful, why do I feel like a fake?* New York: St. Martin's Press.

Ho, R. (1981). Sex, sex-role typing, and children's problem-solving behavior. *Journal of Social Psychology, 115,* 219-226.

Hobbs, N. (1975). *The futures of children.* San Francisco: Jossey-Bass.

Hoffman, L. W. (1972). Early childhood experiences and women's achievement motives. *Journal of Social Issues, 28,* 129-155.

Hollingworth, L. A. (1926). *Gifted children: Their nature and nurture.* New York: Macmillan.

Hollingworth, L. S. (1942). *Children above 180 IQ Stanford-Binet.* Yonkers-on-Hudson, New York: World Book.

Hyde, J. S. (1981). How large are cognitive gender differences? A meta-analysis using w² and d. *American Psychologist, 36,* 892-901.

Jacobs, J. C. (1971). Effectiveness of teacher and parent identification of gifted children as a function of school level. *Psychology in the Schools, VIII,* no. 2, 140-142.

Janos, P. M., Fung, H. C., & Robinson, N. M. (1985). Self-concept, self-esteem, and peer relations among gifted children who feel "different." *Gifted Child Quarterly, 29*(2), 79-82.

Janos, P. M., Marwood, K. A., & Robinson, N. M. (1985). Friendship patterns in highly intelligent children. *Roeper Review, 8*(1), 46-49.

Jeffrey, W. E. (1980). The developing brain and child development. In M. C. Wittrock (Ed.), *The brain and psychology* (pp. 345-370). New York: Academic Press.

Jenkins, R. C. W. (1979). *A resource guide to preschool and primary programs for the gifted and talented.* Mansfield, CT: Creative Learning Press, Inc.

Johnson, S. (1976). *Effect of practice and training in spatial skills on sex related differences in performance on embedded figures.* Unpublished master's thesis. George Mason University, Fairfax, VA.

Jung, C. G. (1938). *Psychological types or the psychology of individuation* (H. G. Baynes, Trans.). London: Kegan Paul, Trench, Trubner & Co., Ltd.

Kagan, J., & Moss, H. A. (1962). *Birth to maturity: A study in psychological development.* New York: Wiley.

Karnes, M. B. (Ed.). (1983). *The underserved: Our young gifted children.* Reston, VA: The Council for Exceptional Children.

Karnes, M. B. (1984a). Nurturing the talented/gifted/pre-school handicapped. *Early Years/K-8, 15*(2), 57-64.

Karnes, M. B. (1984b, September-October). Special children . . . special gifts. *Children Today,* pp. 18-23.

Karnes, M. B., & Associates. (1978). *Nurturing talent guides* (8 vols.). Manuals in the areas of intellectual, academic (reading, math, and science), creative, leadership, visual and performing arts (art and music) and psychomotor talent. Mimeograph. Urbana, IL: Institute for Child Behavior and Development, University of Illinois.

Karnes, M. B., & Bertschi, J. D. (1978). Identifying and educating gifted/talented nonhandicapped and handicapped preschoolers. *Teaching Exceptional Children, 10*(4), 114-119.

Karnes, M. B., Kemp, P., & Williams, M. (1983). Conceptual models. In M. B. Karnes (Ed.), *The underserved: Our young gifted children* (pp. 40-60). Reston, VA: Council for Exceptional Children.

Karnes, M. B., Shwedel, A. M., & Kemp, B. (1985). Preschool programming for the young gifted child. *Roeper Review, 7*(4), 204-209.

Karnes, M. B., Shwedel, A. M., & Lewis, G. F. (1983a). Long-term effects of early programming for the gifted/talented handicapped. *Journal for the Education of the Gifted, 6*(4), 266-278.

Karnes, M. B., Shwedel, A. M., & Lewis, G. F. (1983b). Short-term effects of early programming for the young gifted handicapped child. *Exceptional Children , 50*(2), 103-109.

Karnes, M. B., Shwedel, A. M., Lewis, G. F., Ratts, D. A., & Esry, D. R. (1981). Impact of early programming for the handicapped: A follow-up study into the elementary school. *Journal of the Division for Early Childhood, 4*(1), 62-79.

Karnes, M. B., Shwedel, A. M., & Linnemeyer, S. A. (1981). *Survey of programs for the gifted at the preschool level.* Unpublished manuscript. Urbana, IL: Institute for Child Behavior and Development, University of Illinois.

Karnes, M. B., Shwedel, A. M., & Linnemeyer, S. A. (1982). The young gifted/talented child: Programs at the University of Illinois. *The Elementary School Journal, 8*(3), 195-213.

Karnes, M. B., Shwedel, A. M., & Williams, M. B. (1983, Spring). Combining instructional models for young gifted children. *Teaching Exceptional Children,* pp. 128-135.

Karnes, M. B., Steinberg, D., Brown, J. G., & Shwedel, A. M. (1982). *RAPYHT Talent Assessment Preschool Programming.* Mimeograph. Urbana, IL: Institute for Child Behavior and Development, University of Illinois.

Kiersey, D., & Bates, M. (1978). *Please understand me: Character & temperament types.* Del Mar, CA: Prometheus Nemesis Books.

Kelly, K. R., & Colangelo, N. (1984). Academic and social self-concepts of gifted, general, and special students. *Exceptional Children, 50*(6), 551-554.

Kennell, J., & Klaus, M. (1979). Early mother-infant contact: Effects on the mother and the infant. *Bulletin of the Menninger Clinic*, *43*(1), 69-78.

Kirk, S. A. (1958). *Early education of the mentally retarded*. Urbana, IL: University of Illinois Press.

Kitano, M. K. (1985a). Ethnography of a preschool for the gifted: What gifted young children actually do. *Gifted Child Quarterly*, *29*(2), 67-71.

Kitano, M. K. (1985b). *Needs of gifted preschoolers: Evolution of a concept*. Manuscript submitted for publication.

Kitano, M. K., & Kirby, D. F. (in press-a). *Gifted education: A comprehensive view*. Boston: Little, Brown & Co.

Kitano, M. K., & Kirby, D. F. (in press-b). The unit approach to curriculum planning for the gifted. *G/C/T*.

Kranz, B. (1975). From Lewis Terman to Martina Horner: What happens to gifted girls. *Talent and Gifts, 17*(3), 31-36.

Krech, D. (1969). Psychoneurobiochemeducation. *Phi Delta Kappan, 1*, 370-375.

Lamaze, F. (1970). *Painless childbirth: Psychoprophylactic method* (L. Celestin, Trans.). Chicago: Henry Regnery.

Lazar, I., & Darlington, R. (1979). *Lasting effects after preschool*. U.S. Department of Health and Human Services, Youth, and Families. DHEW Publication No. (OHDS) 80-30-179. Washington, DC: Government Printing Office.

LeBoyer, F. (1975). *Birth without violence*. New York: Random House.

Lehman, E. B., & Erdwins, C. J. (1981). The social and emotional adjustment of young, intellectually gifted children. *Gifted Child Quarterly*, *25*(3), 134-137.

Lemkau, J. P. (1983). Women in male-dominated professions: Distinguishing personality and background characteristics. *Psychology of Women Quarterly*, *8*, 144-165.

Levy, J. (1980). Cerebral asymmetry and the psychology of man. In M. Wittrock (Ed.), *The brain and psychology* (pp. 245-321). New York: Academic Press.

Lewis, M. (1972). Parents and children: Sex role development. *School Review*, *80*, 229-240.

Lewis, M. (1972). State as an infant-environment interaction: An analysis of mother-infant behavior as a function of sex. *Merrill-Palmer Quarterly*, *18*, 95-121.

Lewis, M., & Rosenblum, L. (1974). *The effect of the infant on its caregiver*. New York: Wiley.

Lewis, M., Young, G., Brooks, J., & Michelson, L. (1975). The beginning of friendship. In M. Lewis & L. A. Rosenblum (Eds.), *Friendship and peer relations* (pp. 27-66). New York: John Wiley & Sons.

Licht, B. G., & Dweck, C. S. (1984). Determinants of academic achievement: Interaction of children's achievement orientations with skill area. *Developmental Psychology*, *20*, 628-636.

Lozanov, G. (1977). A general theory of suggestion in the communications process and the activation of the total reserves of the learner's personality. *Suggestopaedia-Canada*, *1*, 1-4.

Luria, A. R. (1973). *The working brain: An introduction to neuropsychology* (B. Haigh, Trans.). New York: Basic Books.

Maccoby, E. E., & Jacklin, C. N. (1974). *The psychology of sex differences*. Stanford, CA: Stanford University Press.

MacLean, P. (1979). A mind of three minds: Educating the triune brain. In J. Chall & A. Mirsky (Eds.), *Education and the brain*, The seventy-seventh yearbook of the National Society for the Study of Education, Part II, pp. 308-342. Chicago: University of Chicago Press.

Maker, C. J. (1977). *Providing programs for the gifted handicapped*. Reston, VA: Council for Exceptional Children.

Marland, S. (1972). *Education of the gifted and talented*. Report to the Subcommittee on Education, Committee on Labor and Public Welfare, U.S. Senate, Washington, D.C.

Martindale, C. (1975). What makes creative people different? *Psychology Today*, *9*(2), 44-50.

Meltzoff, A., & Moore, M. (1977). Imitation of facial and manual gestures by human neonates. *Science*, *198*, 75-78.

Millay, J. (1981, June). A talk given at the New Age School, Pasadena, CA.

Miller, A. (1981). *The drama of the gifted child* (Originally published as *Prisoners of childhood*) (R. Ward, Trans.). New York: Basic Books.

Montour, K. (1977). William James Sidis, the broken twig. *American Psychologist*, *32*, 265-279.

Moore, R. S., Moon, R. D., & Moore, D. R. (1972). The California report: Early schooling for all? *Phi Delta Kappan*, *53*(10), 615-621, 677.

Myers, I. (1962). *Manual: The Myers-Briggs type indicator*. Palo Alto, CA: Consulting Psychologists Press.

Naditch, S. F. (1976, September). *Sex differences in field depen-*

dence: The role of social influence. Paper presented at the meeting of the American Psychological Association, Washington, D.C.

Newland, T. E. (1976). *The gifted in socioeducational perspective.* Englewood Cliffs, NJ: Prentice-Hall.

O'Brien, M., Huston, A. C., & Risley, T. R. (1983). Sex-typed play of toddlers in a day-care center. *Journal of Applied Developmental Psychology, 4,* 1-9.

O'Shea, H. (1960). Friendships and the intellectually gifted child. *Exceptional Children, 26,* 327-335.

Parsons, J. E., Ruble, D. N., Hodges, K. L., & Small, A. W. (1976). Cognitive-developmental factors in emerging sex differences in achievement-related expectancies. *Journal of Social Issues, 32,* 47-61.

Paulus, P. (1984). Acceleration: More than grade skipping. *Roeper Review, 7*(2), 98-100.

Pegnato, C., & Birch, J. (1959). Locating gifted children in junior high school: A comparison of methods. *Exceptional Children, 25,* 300-304.

Pribram, K. (1978). Modes of central processing in human learning and remembering. In T. Teyler (Ed.), *Brain and learning.* Stamford, CT: Greylock.

Pringle, M. O. K. (1970). *Able misfits.* London: Longman.

Project EFFECT Newsletter. (1984). *Roots of Project EFFECT: NIE Research on the Nation's Elementary and Secondary Schools* (Vol. I, No. 1). The American University, Washington, D.C.: Author.

Purkey, W. W. (1984). *Inviting school success* (2nd ed.). Belmont, CA: Wadsworth Publishing.

Renzulli, J., & Hartman, R. (1971). Scale for rating behavioral characteristics of superior students. *Exceptional Children, 38,* 243-248.

Restak, K. (1979). *The brain: The last frontier.* New York; Doubleday.

Roedell, W. C. (1985). Developing social competence in gifted preschool children. *Remedial and Special Education, 6*(4), 6-11.

Roedell, W. C., Jackson, N. E., & Robinson, H. B. (1980). *Gifted young children.* New York: Teachers College Press, Columbia University.

Rosenzweig, M. (1966). Environmental complexity, cerebral change and behavior. *American Psychologist, 21,* 321-332.

Rubin, J. Z., Provenzano, F. J., & Luria, Z. L. (1974). The eye of the beholder: Parents' views on sex of newborns. *American Journal of Orthopsychiatry, 44*, 512-519.

Sadker, M., & Sadker, D. (1985). Sexism in the schoolroom of the 80's. *Psychology Today, 19*(3), 54-57.

Sanford, N. (1956). Personality development during the college years. *Journal of Social Issues, 12*(4), 3-70.

Schlichter, C. (1985, January). Help students become active thinkers. *Early Years/K-8*, 38- 44.

Schweinhart, L. J., & Weikart, D. P. (1980). *The effects of the Perry Preschool Project on youth through age fifteen.* Ypsilanti, MI: High/Scope Press.

Serbin, L. A., O'Leary, K. D., Kent, R. N., & Tonick, I. J. (1973). A comparison of teacher responses to the preacademic and problem behavior of boys and girls. *Child Development, 44*, 796-804.

Shaw, M. C., & McCuen, J. T. (1960). The onset of academic underachievement in bright children. *Journal of Educational Psychology, 51*, 103-108.

Shepard, M. J. (1984). Learning Disabilities. *Special education: Commonalities and controversies.* Conference of Public and Non-Public Schools, City University of New York.

Shwedel, A. M., & Stoneburner, R. (1983). Identification. In M. B. Karnes (Ed.), *The underserved: Our young gifted children.* Reston, VA: The Council for Exceptional Children.

Silverman, L. K. (in press). What happens to the gifted girl? In C. J. Maker (Ed.), *Critical issues in gifted Education.* Rockville, MD: Aspen Systems Corporation.

Silverman, L. K. (1986-a, Feb.). The IQ controversy: Conceptions and misconceptions. *Roeper Review, 8*(3), 136-140.

Silverman, L. K. (in preparation-a). *Gifted education: A developmental approach.* Columbus: Charles E. Merrill.

Silverman, L. K. (in preparation-b). Hunting the hidden culprit in underachievement: Is it ear infections? *G/C/T.*

Silverman, L. K., Chitwood, D. G., & Waters, J. L. (1986-b, Spring). Young gifted children: Can parents identify giftedness? *Topics in Early Childhood Special Education, 6*(1).

Smith, C., & Lloyd, B. (1978). Maternal behavior and perceived sex of infant: Revisited. *Child Development, 49*, 1263-1265.

Spivack, G., & Shure, M. B. (1974). *Special adjustment of young children.* San Francisco: Jossey-Bass.

Sternberg, R. (in press). *Conceptions of giftedness.* New York: Teachers College Press.

Sternberg, R. (1985). *Beyond IQ.* Cambridge: Cambridge University Press.

Stockard, J., & Wood, J. W. (1984). The myth of female underachievement: A reexamination of sex differences in academic underachievement. *American Educational Research Journal, 21,* 825-838.

Stone, L. J., & Church, J. (1973). *Childhood & adolescence: A psychology of the growing person* (3rd ed.). New York: Random House.

Sutherland, A., & Goldschmidt, M. L. (1974). Negative teacher expectation and change in children with superior intellectual potential. *Child Development, 45,* 852-856.

Tannenbaum, A. J. (1983). *Gifted children: Psychological and educational perspectives.* New York: Macmillan.

Terman, L. M. (1926). *Genetic studies of genius* (Vol. 1, 2nd ed.). Stanford, CA: Stanford University Press.

Terman, L. M. (1925). The mental and physical traits of a thousand gifted children. In L. M. Terman (Ed.), *Genetic studies of genius: Mental and physical traits of a thousand gifted children* (Vol. 1). Stanford, CA: Stanford University Press.

Terman, L. M., & Merrill, M. A. (1973). *Stanford-Binet Intelligence Scale manual for the third revision, form L-M.* Boston: Houghton Mifflin.

Terman, L. M., & Odom, M. N. (1959). *Genetic studies of genius. The gifted group at mid-life: Thirty-five years' follow-up of the superior child* (Vol. 5). Stanford, CA: Stanford University Press.

Terrassier, J. C. (1979). Gifted children and psychopathology: The syndrome of dyssynchrony. In J. J. Gallagher (Ed.)., *Gifted children: Reaching their potential.* Proceedings of the Third International Conference on Gifted Children. Jerusalem, Israel: Kollet & Sons.

Thomas, A., & Chess, S. (1977). *Temperament and development.* New York: Brunner/Mazel.

Thompson, R., Berger, T., & Berry, S. (1980). An introduction to the anatomy, physiology, and chemistry of the brain. In M. Wittrock (Ed.), *The brain and psychology.* New York: Academic Press.

Thorndike, R. L. (1985). Mr. Binet's Test—80 Years Later. *Sym-*

posium on cognition and giftedness. Teachers College, Columbia University, New York.

Thorndike, R. L., & Hagen, E. (1977). *Measurement and evaluation in psychology and education* (4th ed.). New York: John Wiley.

Tobin, P. (1982). *The effects of practice and training on sex differences in performance on a spatial task.* Unpublished master's thesis, University of Toronto, Toronto, Canada.

Torrance, E. P. (1981). *Thinking creatively in action and movement.* Bensenville, IL: Scholastic Testing Service, Inc.

Tuddenham, R. D. (1952). Studies in reputation: I. Sex and grade differences in school children's evaluation of their peers. II. The diagnosis of social adjustment. *Psychological Monographs, 66,* No. 333.

VanTassal-Baska, J., Schuler, A., & Lipschutz, J. (1982). An experimental program for gifted four year olds. *Journal for the Education of the Gifted, 5*(1), 45-55.

Verny, T. (1981). *The secret life of the unborn child.* New York: Summit Books.

Webster's *Seventh New Collegiate Dictionary.* (1972). Springfield, MA: G & C Merriam Company.

White, B. K., & Watts, J. C. (1973). *Experience and environment: Vol. 1.* Englewood Cliffs, NJ: Prentice-Hall.

White, B. (1975). *The first three years of life.* Englewood Cliffs, NJ: Prentice-Hall.

Whitmore, J. R. (1978). Characteristics and causes of underachievement in young gifted children. *Roeper Publications* (now *Roeper Review*), *12*(3), 2-6.

Whitmore, J. R. (1979a). Social studies: The lifeblood of education for the gifted. *Social Education, 43*(2), 159-162.

Whitmore, J. R. (1979b). The etiology of underachievement in highly gifted young children. *Journal for the Education of the Gifted, 3*(1), 38-51.

Whitmore, J. R. (1980). *Giftedness, conflict, and underachievement.* Boston: Allyn & Bacon.

Whitmore, J. R. (1983). Changes in teacher education: The key to survival for gifted education. *Roeper Review: A Journal on Gifted Education, 2*(1), 8-13.

Whitmore, J. R. (1984). *Evaluating educational programs for intellectually gifted students* (EEPIGS). New York: United Educational Services.

Whitmore, J. R., & Maker, C. J. (1985). *Intellectual giftedness in disabled persons.* Rockville, MD: Aspen.

Wittrock, M. C. (1980). Learning and the brain. In M. C. Wittrock (Ed.), *The brain and psychology* (pp. 371-403). New York: Academic Press.

Yarrow, L., Rubenstein, J., & Pedersen, F. (1973). *Infant and environment. Early cognitive and motivational development.* New York: Halsted.

Zimmerman, J. (1982). MEG gets inside your head. *Psychology Today, 16*(4), 100.

SELECTED READINGS

ERIC Documents and Journal Articles

ERIC DOCUMENTS

GUIDELINES FOR DEVELOPING A PRESCHOOL LEVEL GIFTED PROGRAM IN THE PRIVATE SECTOR. Doyleen McMurtry. (ED 252 277, 1984, 247p.)

This practicum addresses the creation of an economically viable school in the private sector to meet the educational and social needs of cognitively accelerated preschool-age children. Anticipated outcomes included development of a well-documented philosophical approach, curriculum guidelines for preschool gifted children, and a case study of the process of establishing a preschool/day care center.

IDENTIFICATION AND NURTURANCE OF THE INTELLECTUALLY GIFTED YOUNG CHILD WITHIN THE REGULAR CLASSROOM (AND) CASE HISTORIES. Cheryl A. Wildauer. (ED 254 041, 1984, 178p.)

Examines three case studies of intellectually gifted young children and explores competencies for accurately identifying and nurturing the young gifted child in the regular classroom. The discussion provides a discussion of child development principles and the young gifted child's behaviors in other domains; selected research is also reviewed.

MOTHERS AND GIFTED PRESCHOOLERS: TEACHING AND LEARNING STRATEGIES. Ellen Sheiner Moss. (ED 230 312, 1983, 35p.)

Compares the teaching strategies of mothers of 14 gifted preschoolers with those of mothers of same-age nongifted children. On the basis of videotaped observations, it was concluded that mothers of gifted preschoolers more frequently helped their children structure tasks as goal-directed operations, highlighted perceptual and functional cues to aid feature detection, and encouraged metacognition.

A PRESCHOOL FOR DEVELOPMENTALLY ADVANCED (GIFTED) CHILDREN. Corless McCallister and others. (ED 249 745, 1984, 21p.)

Describes a model summer program for developmentally advanced preschoolers. An open classroom approach involved art, music, dance, and drama activities to encourage creative growth; reading, math, and science taught in an exploratory way; an individualized motor development program; and parent education.

A TEACHER'S GUIDE FOR PROJECT STEP: STRATEGIES FOR TARGETING EARLY POTENTIAL. (ED 254 015, 1984, 27p.)

This manual describes implementation of Project STEP, a program designed to identify potentially gifted minority children in kindergarten and first grade. The objective was to provide an enriched educational program that would help to identify students whose language, cultural, or economic differences may limit the validity of traditional gifted identification measures.

THE UNDERSERVED: OUR YOUNG GIFTED CHILDREN. Merle B. Karnes, editor. (ED 235 645, 1983, 238p.)

Papers contributed by nine authors focus on the needs of preschool gifted and talented children. Among the topics discussed are the challenge of educating this population; identification and conceptual models; characteristics, selection, and training of teachers; differentiated curricula; gifted children's social and affective development; creativity and play; the influence of parent attitudes and behaviors; and evaluation of preschool gifted programs.

JOURNAL ARTICLES

COMPARISON OF THE PERFORMANCE OF GIFTED CHILDREN ON THE McCARTHY SCALES OF CHILDREN'S ABILITIES AND THE STANFORD-BINET INTELLIGENCE SCALE. Bruce A. Bracken. *Journal for the Education of the Gifted*, 1983, *6*(4), 289-93.

Compare the McCarthy Scales with the Stanford-Binet as instruments for identifying and assessing intellectually gifted preschool and primary-age children. The McCarthy Scales consistently produced lower scores than the Binet; low to moderate correlations existed between the two scales.

GIFTED PRESCHOOLERS: EDUCATIONAL IMPLICATIONS OF EARLY IDENTIFICATION. *Special Education in Canada*, 1984, *58*(4), 122-24.

Notes difficulties facing the development of gifted programs for preschoolers, including problems in identification, and discusses four alternatives: regular preschool placement, second-grade placement for some part of the day, regular class placement with time for independent work, and preschool gifted class placement.

PARENTAL PERCEPTIONS OF A PRESCHOOL GIFTED PROGRAM IN A PUBLIC SCHOOL SYSTEM. F. Neil Mathews. *Roeper Review*, 1984, *6*(4), 210-13.

Parents of preschool gifted children were surveyed regarding their attitudes toward the identification process (almost half were uncertain about the system), participation in the program (transportation difficulties), administrative considerations, preschool teachers, and individual planning.

STARTING AN INTERAGE FULL TIME GIFTED CLASS.
Naomi Mirsky. *G/C/T*, 1984, *33*, 24-26.

Describes the formation of a self-contained interage class for
gifted children in first through third grades. The curriculum was
project- and interst-based, and an effort was made to avoid the
charge of elitism by involving other teachers and students.

USE OF SELF-INSTRUCTIONAL MATERIALS WITH GIFTED
PRIMARY-AGED STUDENTS. Beverly N. Parke. *Gifted Child
Quarterly*, 1983, *27*(1), 29-34.

Found that 22 high-achieving students in kindergarten through
second grade who participated in a self-instructional mathematics
program showed greater gains at each level than a high-achieving
control group and a random comparison group. Advantages of self-
instruction included ease of administration, flexibility, and a systematic approach.

WHAT IS YOUR STYLE? A LEARNING STYLES INVEN-
TORY FOR LOWER ELEMENTARY STUDENTS. *Roeper
Review*, 1984, *6*(4), 208-10.

A learning styles inventory listing 27 different classroom tasks in
nine categories (including projects, acting, drill, and peer teaching)
was administered to primary and intermediate students. Subjects
designated by their teachers as gifted indicated preferences different
from those of students designated as nongifted.

ABOUT ERIC

ERIC, the Educational Resources Information Center, is funded
by the National Institute of Education. Included in the ERIC system
are 16 separate clearinghouses, each responsible for collecting and
disseminating information on a specific area in education. The
ERIC Clearinghouse on Elementary and Early Childhood Education
(ERIC/EECE) deals with information relating to the education and
development of children from birth through age 12.

ERIC DOCUMENTS are cited and abstracted in the monthly index *Resources in Education (RIE)*. Most ERIC documents may be read on microfiche in libraries and information centers. In addition, the majority can be ordered in paper copy and/or on microfiche from the ERIC Document Reproduction Service, 3900 Wheeler Ave., Alexandria VA 22304 (Telephone: 800-227-3742).

JOURNAL ARTICLES are cited and annotated in the monthly publication *Current Index to Journals in Education (CIJE)*; journals may be read at libraries or ordered through subscription. Selected article reprints are available from University Microfilms International, Article Clearinghouse, 300 N. Zeeb Rd., Ann Arbor, MI 48106 (Telephone: 800-732-0616). Please contact UMI or see the most recent issue of *CIJE* for ordering details.

Further information about the ERIC network and services of ERIC/EECE is available from ERIC/EECE Information Services, University of Illinois, 805 W. Pennsylvania Ave., Urbana, IL 61801 (Telephone: 217-333-1386).

APPENDIXES

APPENDIX 1: From *Growing Up Gifted*, Second Edition, (pp 91-99) by B. Clark, 1983, Columbus, Ohio: Charles E. Merrill Publishing Co. Copyright 1983 by Charles E. Merrill. Reprinted by permission.

Table 2.5. Differential Cognitive (Thinking) Characteristics of the Gifted.

Cognitive development rests on the analysis, integration, and evaluation of a vast quantity of experiences of the environment and understandings of those experiences. Educational programs should provide for an array of such experiences and encourage the processes of understanding, analyzing, organizing, integrating, and evaluating. Qualitatively different planning for the gifted implies recognition of the ways in which their differential cognitive characteristics affect this process.

Differentiating Characteristics	Examples of Related Needs	Possible Concomitant Problems
Extraordinary quantity of information, unusual retentiveness	To be exposed to new and challenging information of the environment and the culture, including aesthetic, economic, political, educational, and social aspects; to acquire early mastery of foundation skills	Boredom with regular curriculum; impatience with "waiting for the group"
Advanced comprehension	Access to challenging curriculum and intellectual peers	Poor interpersonal relationships with less able children of the same age; adults considering children "sassy" or "smart alec;" a dislike for repetition of already understood concepts
Unusually varied interests and curiosity	To be exposed to varied subjects and concerns; to be allowed to pursue individual ideas as far as interest takes them	Difficulty in conforming to group tasks; overextending energy levels, taking on too many projects at one time
High level of language development	To encounter uses for increasingly difficult vocabulary and concepts	Perceived as a "show off" by children of the same age
High level of verbal ability	To share ideas verbally in depth	Dominate discussions with information and questions deemed negative by teachers and fellow students; use of verbalism to avoid difficult thinking tasks

APPENDIX 1, continued

Table 2.5. Differential Cognitive (Thinking) Characteristics of the Gifted. *(continued)*

Differentiating Characteristics	Examples of Related Needs	Possible Concomitant Problems
Unusual capacity for processing information	To be exposed to ideas at many levels and in large variety	Resents being interrupted; perceived as too serious; dislike for routine and drill
Accelerated pace of thought processes	To be exposed to ideas at rates appropriate to individual pace of learning	Frustration with inactivity and absence of progress
Flexible thought processes	To be allowed to solve problems in diverse ways	Seen as disruptive and disrespectful to authority and tradition
Comprehensive synthesis	To be allowed a longer incubation time for ideas	Frustration with demands for deadlines and for completion of each level prior to starting new inquiry
Early ability to delay closure	To be allowed to pursue ideas and integrate new ideas without forced closure or products demanded	If products are demanded as proof of learning, will refuse to pursue an otherwise interesting subject or line of inquiry
Heightened capacity for seeing unusual and diverse relationships	To mess around with varieties of materials and ideas	Frustration at being considered "off the subject" or irrelevant in pursuing inquiry in areas other than that subject being considered; considered odd or weird by others
Ability to generate original ideas and solutions	To build skills in problem solving and productive thinking; opportunity to contribute to solution to meaningful problems	Difficulty with rigid conformity; may be penalized for not following directions; may deal with rejection by becoming rebellious

Table 2.5. Differential Cognitive (Thinking) Characteristics of the Gifted. *(continued)*

Differentiating Characteristics	Examples of Related Needs	Possible Concomitant Problems
Early differential patterns for thought processing (e.g., thinking in alternatives, abstract terms, sensing consequences, making generalizations)	To be exposed to alternatives, abstractions, consequences of choices, and opportunities for drawing generalizations and testing them	Rejection or omission of detail: questions generalizations of others, which may be perceived as disrespectful behavior
Early ability to use and form conceptual frameworks	To use and to design conceptual frameworks in information gathering and problem solving; to seek order and consistency; to develop a tolerance for ambiguity	Frustration with inability of others to understand or appreciate original organizations or insights: personally devised systems or structure may conflict with procedures of systems later taught
An evaluative approach to themselves and others	To be exposed to individuals of varying ability and talent, and to varying ways of seeing and solving problems; to set realistic, achievable short-term goals: to develop skills in data evaluation and decision making	Perceived by others as elitist, conceited, superior, too critical: may become discouraged from self-criticism, can inhibit attempting new areas if fear of failure is too great: seen by others as too demanding, compulsive: can affect interpersonal relationships as others fail to live up to standards set by gifted individual: intolerant of stupidity
Persistent, goal-directed behavior	To pursue inquires beyond allotted time spans, to set and evaluate priorities	Perceived as stubborn, willful, uncooperative

APPENDIX 1, continued

Table 2.6. Differential Affective (Feeling) Characteristics of the Gifted.

High levels of cognitive development do not necessarily imply high levels of affective development. The same heightened sensitivities that underlie gifted intelligence can contribute to an accumulation of information about emotions that the student needs to process. The affect-based information comes from sources within and without the child. Gifted children need to learn that their cognitive powers applied to this material will help them to make sense of their world. Their educational program must provide opportunities to bring emotional knowledge and assumptions to awareness, and to apply verbal ability and inquiry skills in the service of affective development.

The early appearance of social conscience that often characterizes gifted children signals an earlier need for development of a value structure and for the opportunity to translate values into social action. This can occur in the context of the society of the classroom and should then be extended into the larger world, as appropriate to the child's increasing competence and widening concerns.

Differentiating Characteristics	Examples of Related Needs	Possible Concomitant Problems
Large accumulation of information about emotions, that has not been brought to awareness	To process cognitively the emotional meaning of experience, to name one's own emotions, to identify one's own and others' perceptual filters and defense systems, to expand and clarify awareness of the physical environment, to clarify awareness of the needs and feelings of others	Information misinterpreted affecting the individual negatively
Unusual sensitivity to the expectations and feelings of others	To learn to clarify the feelings and expectations of others	Unusually vulnerable to criticism of others, high level of need for success and recognition
Keen sense of humor—may be gentle or hostile	To learn how behaviors affect the feelings and behaviors of others	Use of humor for critical attack upon others resulting in damage to interpersonal relationships
Heightened self-awareness, accompanied by feelings of being different	To learn to assert own needs and feelings nondefensively, to share self with others, for self-clarification	Isolate self; resulting in being considered aloof; feeling rejected; perceive difference as a negative attribute resulting in low self-esteem and inhibited growth emotionally and socially

APPENDIX 1, continued

Table 2.6. Differential Affective (Feeling) Characteristics of the Gifted. *(continued)*

Differentiating Characteristics	Examples of Related Needs	Possible Concomitant Problems
Idealism and sense of justice, which appear at an early age	To transcend negative reactions by finding values to which he or she can be committed	Attempt unrealistic reforms and goals with resulting intense frustration (Suicides result from intense depression over issues of this nature.)
Earlier development of an inner locus of control and satisfaction	To clarify personal priorities among conflicting values; To confront and interact with the value system of others	Difficulty conforming; reject external validation and choose to live by personal values that may be seen as a challenge to authority or tradition
Unusual emotional depth and intensity	To find purpose and direction from personal value system; To translate commitment into action in daily life	Unusual vulnerability; problem focusing on realistic goals for life's work
High expectations of self and others, often leading to high levels of frustration with self, others, and situations; Perfectionism	To learn to set realistic goals and to accept setbacks as part of the learning process; To hear others express their growth in acceptance of self	Discouragement and frustration from high levels of self-criticism; problems maintaining good interpersonal relations as others fail to maintain high standards imposed by gifted individual; immobilization of action due to high levels of frustration resulting from situations that do not meet expectations of excellence
Strong need for consistency between abstract values and personal actions	To find a vocation that provides opportunity for actualization of student's personal value system, as well as an avenue for his or her talents and abilities	Frustration with self and others leading to inhibited actualization of self and interpersonal relationships
Advanced levels of moral judgment	To receive validation for nonaverage morality	Intolerance of and lack of understanding from peer group, leading to rejection and possible isolation

APPENDIX 1, continued

Table 2.7. Differential Physical (Sensation) Characteristics of the Gifted.

People of highly developed intellectual ability may be unusually vulnerable to a characteristic "Cartesian split" between thinking and being; a lack of integration between mind and body. During school years, when the gifted student is experiencing large discrepancies between physical and intellectual development, the school may be unintentionally encouraging the student to avoid physical activity. If a child's intellectual peers are physically more advanced so as to make him or her feel physically inadequate, while physical peers are less intellectually stimulating and not within his or her friendship group, the usual competitive playground games may be neither inviting nor satisfying to the gifted child. If the physical development of the gifted child is to be encouraged, programs should provide experiences that develop integration between mind and body in children with nonnormative development patterns.

Differentiating Characteristics	Examples of Related Needs	Possible Concomitant Problems
Unusual quantity of input from the environment through a heightened sensory awareness	To engage in activities that will allow integration and assimilation of sensory data	Attention moving diffusely toward many areas of interest; overexpenditure of energy due to lack of integration; seeming disconnectedness
Unusual discrepancy between physical and intellectual development	To appreciate their physical capacities	Result in gifted adults who function with a mind/body dichotomy; gifted children who are only comfortable expressing themselves in mental activity, resulting in a limited development both physically and mentally
Low tolerance for the lag between their standards and their athletic skills	To discover physical activities as a source of pleasure; to find satisfaction in small increments of improvement; to engage in noncompetitive physical activities	Refuse to take part in any activities where they do not excel; limiting their experience with otherwise pleasurable, constructive physical activities
"Cartesian split"—can include neglect of physical well-being and avoidance of physical activity	To engage in activities leading to mind/body integration; to develop a commitment to own physical well-being; to extend this concern to the social and political realm	Detrimental to full mental and physical health, inhibiting to the development of potential for the individual

166

Table 2.8. Differential Intuitive Characteristics of the Gifted.

This area of the human experience is involved in initiating or insightful acts and in creative activity. While this is the least well-defined area of human endeavor, it is probably the area that promises the most for the continuance and fulfillment of humankind. All other areas provide support for and are supported by this area of function. As each area evolves to high levels, more of the intuitive and creative are available.

Differentiating Characteristics	Examples of Related Needs	Possible Concomitant Problems
Early involvement and concern for intuitive knowing and metaphysical ideas and phenomena	Opportunities to engage in meaningful dialogue with philosophers and others concerned with these ideas; to become aware of own intuitive energy and ability; guidance in developing and using intuitive energy and ability	Ridiculed by peers; not taken seriously by elders; considered weird or strange
Open to experiences in this area; will experiment with psychic and metaphysical phenomena	Guidance in becoming familiar with, analyzing, and evaluating such phenomena; should be provided a historical approach	Can become narrowly focused toward ungrounded belief systems
Creativity apparent in all areas of endeavor	Guidance in evaluating appropriate uses of creative efforts; encouragement for continued development of creative abilities	Seen as deviant; becomes bored with more mundane tasks; may be viewed as troublemaker

APPENDIX 1, continued

Table 2.9. Differential Societal Characteristics of the Gifted.

Society has unique needs for the services of unique individuals. While we would not wish that education for the gifted focus on societal needs at the expense of the needs of these individuals, neither can education of the gifted disregard the importance of their mature social roles. Gifted students need direction in exploring all the opportunities society has to offer them and the ways of contributing what they have to offer to society. They need conceptual frameworks to organize their experience of society (e.g., Maslow's (1968) hierarchy of needs), and they need opportunities to develop those skills that will make it possible for them to affect society. Educational programs should provide for the options, conceptual frameworks, and skills that will underlie effective social involvement of gifted students.

Differentiating Characteristics	Examples of Related Needs	Possible Concomitant Problems
Differential Societal Characteristics of the Gifted		
Strongly motivated by self-actualization needs	Opportunities to follow divergent paths, pursue strong interests, help in understanding the demands of self-actualization	Frustration of not feeling challenged; loss of unrealized talents
Advanced cognitive and affective capacity for conceptualizing and solving societal problems	Encounters with social problems, awareness of the complexity of problems facing society; conceptual frameworks for problem-solving procedures	Tendency for "quick" solutions not taking into account the complexity of the problem; young age of gifted person often makes usable alternatives suspect; older, more experienced decision makers may not take the gifted person seriously.

APPENDIX 1, continued

Table 2.9. Differential Societal Characteristics of the Gifted. *(continued)*

Differentiating Characteristics	Examples of Related Needs	Possible Concomitant Problems
Differential Social Expectations for the Gifted		
Leadership	Understanding of various leadership steps and practice in leadership skills	Lack of opportunity to use this ability constructively may result in its disappearance from child's repertoire or its being turned into a negative characteristic, e.g., gang leadership.
Solutions to social and environmental problems	Meaningful involvement in real problems	Loss to society if these traits are not allowed to develop with guidance and opportunity for meaningful involvement
Involvement with the meta-needs of society (e.g., justice, beauty, truth)	Exploration of the highest levels of human thought; application of this knowledge to today's problems	

Appendix 2

Standardized Tests for Selective Use in Assessing Talent*

Talent Area   Tests Available

Intellectual

      Concept Assessment Kit
         (Goldschmidt & Bentler, 1968)
      Detroit Tests of Learning Aptitude-Revised
         (Hammill, 1984)
      Goodenough-Harris Drawing Test
         (Harris, 1963)
      Kaufman Assessment Battery for Children
         (Kaufman & Kaufman, 1983)
      Leiter International Performance Scale
         (Stoelting, 1952)
      McCarthy Scales of Children's Abilities
         (McCarthy, 1972)
      Pictorial Test of Intelligence
         (French, 1964)
      Raven's Coloured Progressive Matrices
         (Psychological Corporation, 1947)
      Stanford-Binet Intelligence Scale, Form L-M
         (Terman & Merrill, 1973)
      Slosson Intelligence Test
         (Slosson, 1971)
      Wechsler Preschool and Primary Scale of
         Intelligence
         (Wechsler, 1967)
      Wechsler Intelligence Scale for Children--Revised
         (Wechsler, 1974)
      Woodcock-Johnson Psychoeducational Battery, Part I
         (Woodcock & Johnson, 1977)

Achievement-Readiness

      KeyMath Diagnostic Arithmetic Test
         (Connolly, Nachtman, & Pritchett, 1976)
      Metropolitan Readiness Test, Level 1
         (Nurss & McGauvran, 1976)
      Peabody Individual Achievement Test
         (Dunn & Markwardt, 1970)

APPENDIX 2, continued

Stanford Early School Achievement Test, Level
    (Madden & Gardner, 1969)
Test of Basic Experiences, Level K
    (Moss, 1971)
Woodcock-Johnson Psychoeducational Battery,
    Part II
    (Woodcock & Johnson, 1977)
Woodcock Reading Mastery Tests
    (Woodcock, 1973)

Perceptual-Motor Development

Basic Motor Ability Test
    (Arnheim & Sinclair, 1974)
Bender Visual-Motor Gestalt Test
    (Koppitz, 1975)
Developmental Test of Visual-Motor Integration
    (Revised Norms, 1982)
    (Beery, 1967)
Purdue Perceptual-Motor Survey
    (Roach & Kephart, 1966)
Revised Visual Retention Test
    (Benton, 1974)
Wechsler Preschool and Primary Scale of
    Intelligence: Performance Scale
    (Wechsler, 1967)

Social Development

AAMD Adaptive Behavior Scale, School Edition
    (Lambert, 1981)
California Preschool Social Competency Scale
    (Levine, Elzey, & Lewis, 1969)
Vineland Social Maturity Scale
    (Doll, 1965)
Vineland Adaptive Behavior Scales
    (Sparrow, Balla, & Cicchett, 1984)

Creative and Productive Thinking

Creative Thinking: Verbal Test, Forms A & B
    (Torrance, 1966)
The Make-A-Tree Test
    (Ward, 1974-1975/1979)

APPENDIX 2, continued

Tests of Creative Thinking: Figural Tests,
Form A & B
(Torrance, 1966)
Thinking Creatively in Action and Movement
(Research Edition)
(Torrance, 1976)
Self-Concept and Achievement Motivation
Animal Crackers
(Research Education)
(Adkin & Ballif, 1973)
Primary Self-Concept Inventory
(Muller & Leonetti, 1973)
The Self-Concept and Motivation Inventory
(Milchus, Farrah, & Reitz, 1968)
Musical Ability
Seashore Measurement of Musical Talent
(Seashore, Lewis, & Saetveit, 1956;
Rev. ed. 1960)
Tests of Musical Ability and Appreciation
(Herbert Wind, 1968)

*Full information on most of these instruments is available in O. K. Buros
(Ed.), The Mental Measurements Yearbook, 8th ed., (Highland Park, NJ:
Gryphon Press, 1978).

Appendix 3

Components of Giftedness Addressed by States

Intellectual, Academic, Creative, Leadership, Visual and Performing Arts,
Psychomotor

Illinois	Nebraska	Massachusetts	Pennsylvania
Washington, D. C.	Hawaii	Arkansas	Delaware
New Jersey	Colorado	Texas	California

Intellectual, Academic, Creative, Leadership, Visual and Performing Arts

Iowa	Guam	Indiana	Mississippi
Minnesota	Idaho	Montana	Oklahoma
Oregon			

APPENDIX 3, continued

Intellectual, Academic, Leadership, Creative

    Michigan   South Dakota

Intellectual, Academic, Creative, Visual and Performing Arts

    Connecticut   Missouri   Ohio   Rhode Island

    Maryland   Maine

Intellectual, Creative, Leadership, Psychomotor

    West Virginia

Intellectual, Academic, Critical Thinking, Creative

    New Mexico

Intellectual, Academic, Creative, Visual and Performing Arts, Psychomotor,

Vocational Education

    Virginia

Intellectual, Academic, Visual and Performing Arts

    New York

Intellectual, Academic, Creative

    Florida   Kansas   Alaska

Intellectual, Visual and Performing Arts

    Nevada   South Carolina

Intellectual, Academic

    North Carolina   Arizona   Washington   Louisiana

    Georgia

Intellectual

    Tennessee

Appendix 4

State Guidelines for the Identification of Giftedness

States that require an IQ test and/or an academic achievement test with

specific cut-off scores:

    West Virginia   Delaware

    Nebraska   Pennsylvania

    Nevada   Ohio (visual and performing arts exempt)

    Missouri   Mississippi (talented or handicapped/gifted

                           exempt)

States that require a creativity test, an IQ test, and/or an academic

achievement test but do not specify a cut-off score:

    Illinois

APPENDIX 4, continued

States that use a "point system" based on an IQ test, an achievement test, classroom performance, and recommendations:

Florida	North Carolina
South Carolina	Minnesota

States that leave the criteria to the LEA but specify a multi-instrument approach:

Michigan	New York	South Dakota
Washington, D.C.	Colorado	California
Connecticut	Arkansas	Oregon
New Jersey	Rhode Island	Hawaii
Virginia	Maryland	Texas
Maine	Oklahoma	

States that leave the criteria and instrument selection to the LEA:

Massachusetts	Arizona
Alaska	Iowa
Montana	North Dakota

States that strongly suggest IQ, achievement tests, and cut-offs:

Idaho –   3 of 5 assessments must be used:

                  IQ test (98 percentile)

                  academic achievement test (98 percentile)

New Mexico –   2 are necessary:

                  creativity – 1.5 standard deviations or

                        96 percentile

                  IQ – 2 standard deviations

                  critical thinking – 96 percentile

                  achievement – 95 percentile

Kansas –   <u>suggests</u> IQ – 95 percentile

                  achievement – 95 percentile

Index

Adultizing, 86
Achievements vs. Underachievements
  cognitive styles, sex differences,
    108,110
  differential influences, play,
    television, toys, 113-114
  differential treatment, parents,
    111-112
  differential treatment, teachers, 112
  educational right, 106
  environmental influences, 110. *See
    also* Environment
  heredity, 110
  males, 106-107
  mathematical skills, sex differences,
    107
  personality traits, sex differences,
    108-109
  research, 111
  spatial skills, sex differences, 107
  verbal skills, sex differences, 107
  women's movement, 106
  See also Boys, Gifted Girls
Affective education, 130-131,136
  See also Prevention/Intervention of
    Underachievement
Age, identification of giftedness.
  See Identification of giftedness
American Indian children, 63
  See also Gifted Children
Assessment methods. *See* Identification
  of giftedness; Tests
Astor Program. *See* Program Models
Behavior. *See* Achievement vs.
  Underachievement; Gifted Children;
  Underachievement
Behavior problems, 123-124
  boys, gifted, 135
  girls, gifted, 136
Boys. *See* Achievement vs.
  Underachievement; Behavior problems

Brain
  research, 8,10,12,13,15,135
Brain function
  brain stem, 5,12,15
  cortex, 5,12,15
  feeling, 5,12
  integrative process, 10-11
  intuition, 5,12
  limbic system, 5,12,15
  midbrain, 5,12,15
  physical/sensing, 5,12
  prefontal cortex, 5,12,15
  tension, affect on, 11
  thinking, 5,12
  See also Brain, Brain organization,
    Environment, Intelligence
Brain organization
  axon, 6-7
  biochemical influences, 6,12,15
  brain stem, 11-12,15
  cerebrum, 10-11
  corpus collosum, 12
  dendrites, 6-7
  hemispheric specialization, 11-12
  integrative capabilities, 11-12
  integrative process, 10-14. *See also*
    Brain function
  limbic system, 10-11
  neocortex, 10-11
  neuroglial cells, 15
  neurons, 6-7,15
  new mammalian brain, 10-11
  old mammalian brain, 10-11
  prefontal cortex, 11,15
  reptilian brain, 10
  reticular formation, 10
  synaptic process, 6,15
  tension, influence on, 12
  triune brain, 10-11
  See also Brain functions; Environment;
    Intelligence; Learning process

Pressure tactics. *See* Motivation
Prevention/Intervention of
    underachievement
  curriculums, 129-131,135,161-169
  early education, value of, 137-138
  early intervention, 136
  student/teacher relationships, 128
  teacher characteristics, 127-128
  See also Underachievement
Programs
  accelerated programs, 92-94
  age requirements, 36
  assessment/program match, 50
  availability of, 35-36
  enrichment, 94-95
  evaluation guidelines, 100-101
  federally sponsored, 36
  goals/objectives, 95-96,98
  homogeneous/heterogeneous, 90-92
  match programs to child's needs, 96
  organizational structure, 92
  parent involvement, 51
  placement guidelines, 98
  placement options, 95
  policy for programs, 103
  preschool programs, 96,98,106
  principles, 55
  pull-out, 92
  research, 93,97
  social skill development, 97.
    See also Social development
  staffing issues, 36-37
  state legislation, 36
  talented handicapped child, 47-53
  teacher qualifications, 90
  teacher training, 48-49
  See also Curriculums; Identification of
    Giftedness; Prevention/Intervention
    of underachievement; Program
    models
Program models
  Astor program, 57-58,60-62,67-69
  Bringing Out Head Start Talent
    (BOHST), 51
  Cupertino Program for Underachieving
    Gifted Students, 119-120,123,
    131-132

Enrichment Triad Model, 98
Multiple Talent Approach, 98
New Mexico State University
  Preschool for the Gifted, 96
Open Classroom, 98
Retrieval and Acceleration of
  Promising Young Handicapped
  Talented (RAPHYT), 47-48.
  See also Gifted children
Structure of Intellect, 98
The University Primary School, 51-53
Psychological disorders. *See* Emotional
  conflict
Public policy
  Curriculum development, relation to,
    137
  Public Law 94-142, 135
  See also States, support of giftedness
Screening instruments, 49
  See also Identification of giftedness;
    Tests
Self-concepts. *See* Behavior problems;
    Gifted children
Sex differences, 106
  cognitive abilities, 107
  cognitive style, 108,110
  origins of differences, 110-114
  personality differences, 108
Sex role stereotyping, 109
  See also Achievement vs.
    Underachievement; Girls, gifted
Sibling relationships. *See* Gifted
    children; Parents
Social development
  guidelines, 129
  See also Gifted children
Social relationships. *See* Curriculums;
    Gifted children; Prevention/
    Intervention of underachievement
States, support of giftedness, 172-174
Structure of Intellect. *See* Program
    models
Synaptic process. *See* Brain organization;
    Environment
Task avoidance. *See* Underachievement
Teachers
  differential treatment, 112